THE TROUT AND SALMON HANDBOOK

THE TROUT AND SALMON HANDBOOK

Robin Ade
with illustrations by the author

Facts On File
New York • Oxford

Facts On File, Inc.
460 Park Avenue South
New York, New York 10016

Library of Congress Catalog Card Number 88–046177

Typeset by Opus, Oxford
Printed and bound in Great Britain
by Butler & Tanner Ltd., Frome, Somerset

CONTENTS

PREFACE

There can be no happier way of researching a work on fish than by means of angling. It has been my good fortune to do just that. The inspiration and a large part of the information for this book is based on fishing experiences in many countries.

Some of my angling travels have been brief, offering no more than a tantalising glimpse of an area and its fish. Visits to Lapland, the Himalayas or the Caspian watershed of Iran have been all too short. In other places, it has been possible to follow the comings and goings of the fish over the seasons and to know the local streams, lakes or ocean fringes as home waters. The Pacific Northwest and the 'God's Pocket' country of western Canada have given me first-hand experience of the salmon, trout and char of the Pacific basin. The charismatic Hindu Kush mountains of Afghanistan displayed an unexploited wealth of wild brown trout. Wales gave me my first sea trout and Scotland, home of salmon angling traditions, my first Atlantic salmon.

The wielding of a fishing rod could not, however, produce all the information demanded by a book of this kind. In attempting an overview of the world's salmonids it has been necessary to draw on many sources and I gratefully acknowledge the assistance I have received. Special thanks are due to Paul Minns who, apart from his work in designing the book, helped to ensure that its completion was inspired by regular visits to the riverbank. Last season our local waters had their best salmon runs on record and we were lucky enough to get a share of the fish.

This handbook has two main aims. The first is to provide a recognition guide to the salmonids. The worldwide total of species is not large, yet confusion between those from different waters, or at different life stages, can occur even among the best known ones. The second aim is to offer a simple account of their natural history at a time when our rich heritage of wild trout, salmon and char is in ever-increasing need of enlightened management.

ROBIN ADE
SCOTLAND, 1989

INTRODUCTION: THE SALMONIDS

Trout, salmon and their allies comprise a distinctive and closely related group of fish belonging to the salmoniform order. The oldest order of bony fishes, the salmoniforms include numerous ocean species and the freshwater graylings and whitefishes. The latter are sometimes included in the suborder Salmonidae but those dealt with in this guide are limited to the more typical salmonids – the genus *Salmo* (Atlantic salmon and trouts), *Oncorhynchus* (Pacific salmons), *Salvelinus* (chars) and *Hucho* (taimen and huchen).

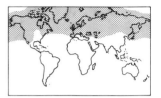

Native range of salmonids. 10,000 years ago, when most of the area was under ice, their range extended further south.

The salmonids are native to the cool fresh waters and oceans of the northern hemisphere. The greatest number of individual species is found in the Pacific basin, which has two or more members of each genus, while the north Atlantic basin has two major species of *Salmo* – the Atlantic salmon and the brown or sea trout – and two chars. The northern land masses of North America and Eurasia are home to the only important species restricted entirely to fresh water – the lake trout (a char) and the taimen, the main representative of the genus *Hucho*.

Basic habitat requirements are similar for all salmonids. They are pollution-sensitive and require pure, cool, well-oxygenated water in which to live and grow. For successful reproduction they need access to gravelly freshwater spawning areas. All are strongly carnivorous and require appropriately sized prey items at different growth stages. The common species are all exploited by man, either for their high-quality food value or the important part they play in angling, the world's largest participant sport. Commercial fishing is nowadays aimed primarily at salmon which are taken on their ocean feeding grounds or the approaches to their parent rivers as they return to spawn. Although salmon fisheries are major providers of food, especially in the Pacific basin where they comprise a large industry, the development of intensive farming has led in recent years to the increased availability of both trout and salmon for human consumption.

Of the people who take a direct interest in the salmonid fish, anglers comprise by far the greatest proportion. As a recreational activity angling is concerned not just with the hunting of fish but with an interest in the natural environment; sport fishermen play a similar part in the conservation of fish to birdwatchers in the conservation of bird life. The current unprecedented threats to freshwater habitats demand an increasingly high level of knowledge and awareness by anglers in the face of water pollution, abstraction or the planting of inappropriate fish species. Good stocks of fish require clean water and a healthy aquatic environment – matters of importance to everyone.

Origins

Our modern salmonids evolved during the Pleistocene age, the era of great ice ages which began 100 million years ago. The fossil record gives scant indication as to which of them developed first; nor does it show whether they evolved in fresh water or the oceans, a question which has led to considerable speculation among biologists.

The case for a freshwater origin is based largely on the fact that all species breed in fresh water and that since there are no wholly marine forms they could not have evolved in the ocean. According to this theory ancestral salmonids developed into the 'primitive' freshwater-dwelling huchens and led on to chars, trout, the Atlantic salmon and finally the Pacific salmons. Moreover detailed geographic evidence appeared to show how, in the last million years, the Atlantic salmon could have given rise to the Pacific salmons. This speculation was discredited however, by the discovery of fossils some five million years old including a giant species of extinct Pacific salmon as well as coho, a living species.

A marine origin makes more sense from the viewpoint of salmonid distribution. This theory assumes their evolution from fish like smelts and argentines, closely related species which often spawn on beaches or the upper tidal limit of river estuaries. Having found the freshwater environment suitable for the protection of their large eggs and for the rearing of their young, salmonids could have progressively colonised river systems via the sea. The differentiation of trout into numerous local freshwater races points to the possibility of a common marine ancestor. A marine origin would also indicate that the Pacific salmons are actually the most 'primitive', being least adapted to a full freshwater existence, and that it is from them or their predecessors that other salmonids developed.

External Features of Salmonid Fish (rainbow trout).

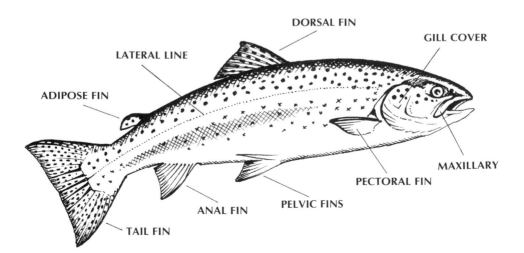

DORSAL FIN

GILL COVER

LATERAL LINE

ADIPOSE FIN

MAXILLARY

PECTORAL FIN

PELVIC FINS

ANAL FIN

TAIL FIN

Life Strategies

One of the most fascinating aspects of the salmonids is the great variety in size, appearance and individual habitat. Two fish from the same brood may grow, reproduce and live for the same number of years, one spending its entire life in a small stream and reaching only a few ounces in weight while the other travels for thousands of miles in the ocean and achieves a weight of many pounds. Such variety is one result of the wide range of life strategy options which help account for the success of these species.

Salmon epitomise their remarkable ability to thrive in both freshwater and ocean environments. Juvenile salmon are common residents of temperate and subarctic streams while adults are major predators of northern oceans. Those with the simplest life cycle are the Pacific pink and sockeye, which spend a fixed time at sea and return at a fairly standard size to spawn in their parent streams. Chum and coho show more variety in adult weights while the chinook and the Atlantic salmon may spend from one to five years at sea, achieving a wide range of sizes and often returning in seasonal stages rather than at one time.

The most complex life strategies are exhibited by trout and char. Individual tributary streams commonly have their own ratios of residents, lake or river migrants, and anadromous (sea-going) fish. Often a lower proportion of males migrate than females, a phenomenon which may be due to the fact that the big eggs produced by big migratory females produce larger and stronger young. Such varied strategies, produced by local environmental conditions, are reinforced over time by the establishment of genetic strains. Most anadromous trout become silver smolts prior to migration, for instance, while those living above impassable falls will entirely lose the instinct to migrate. Such genetic adaptations show why mixed hatchery strains may do less well in the wild than native fish.

An important factor in the success of any species is its relationship with rival salmonids. The main competitor to young Atlantic salmon is the brown trout in Europe and the brook trout in North America. Competition between them is reduced by salmon dominating the faster water and the other species the slower. Such habitat preferences are important considerations when alien species are introduced into a river system. Brown trout and brook trout do not thrive well in the same stream, for instance, nor do rainbow trout and Atlantic salmon. The fact that rainbows and browns can co-exist successfully is probably due to the fact that the brown has a similar habitat preference to the rainbow's natural Pacific neighbour, the cutthroat trout, while the rainbow occupies a similar place to the Atlantic salmon in relation to the brown trout.

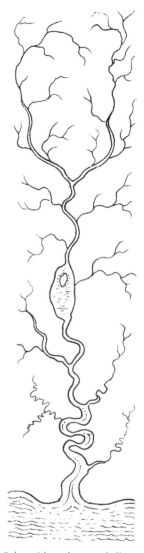

Salmonids make use of all possible habitats. Many species use small headwater streams for spawning and for the rearing of young, lakes and rivers as feeding grounds. Lakes and deep riverpools are also used as shelter by large sea-run adults returning to spawn.

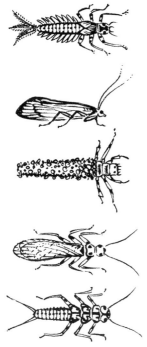

Food and Growth

After hatching, young salmonids, at this stage called alevins, remain deep in the spawning gravels nourished by their yolk sacs. Once this infant food supply is exhausted they emerge from the gravel as tiny, free-swimming fry. At first they school together, feeding on planktonic creatures such as midge and mayfly larvae brought to them by the current. Within weeks most species become territorial, however, and even if food is abundant they will not thrive unless they can acquire suitably sized individual lairs and feeding stations. This stage of their life is critical since, while spawning streams provide numerous lairs among stones, the huge numbers of eggs produced by salmonids result in far more young than most waters can support. On a typical stream over 90 per cent of fry will die in the first months as a direct consequence of territorial competition. A positive result of this is that many drift downstream to fill all appropriate habitats, resulting in the maximum number of young fish establishing themselves. Territorial behaviour and a strict size hierarchy are also maintained among resident older fish, with the largest dominating the best lairs and feeding areas; but big ones will tolerate the company of a number of lesser fish and the net result of territorial behaviour is likely to be a maximum complement of healthy fish of different sizes throughout a river system.

Competition is not the only reason for young fish leaving the pool of their birth. Although a typical rocky, acid spawning stream has enough food creatures to support large numbers of small fish, it will not produce enough for many of them to reach much of a size. Most obey environmental or genetic influences in moving downstream to richer feeding grounds.

In fresh water the best feeding is found in alkaline areas since acidity in water, as in soil, tends to tie up nutrient minerals vital to the food chain. Rivers and lakes lying on chalk or limestone produce a bigger total weight of fish than acid ones of equivalent size and individual growth rates are also higher. Such waters commonly hold a broad range of invertebrate foods – often resulting in selective feeding behaviour – although very large fish are likely to require more substantial fare to maintain growth; they occur both in acid and alkaline habitats and feed mainly on other fish.

The seasons play a significant part in salmonid growth. At low temperatures fish become inactive and any food eaten will take longer to digest; during winter they do little more than maintain themselves in spite of the fact that aquatic foods remain abundant. The main growing season in the northern hemisphere is from April to November when water temperatures are mostly between 5°C (41°F) and 20°C (68°F), the range in which salmonids feed actively enough not only to maintain themselves but to put on weight and develop

Availability is the main factor in choice of prey. Larval and adult forms of mayfly (top), caddis and stonefly are 'bread and butter' for salmonids in stony streams. Terrestrial insects are also important and may account for one third of their stream diet.

Shrimps and similar crustaceans are major food sources in salt water and in many fresh waters.

ovaries and testes. Growth during the summer is rapid even in small streams where, for their first few years, trout commonly triple their weight each growing season. The slowest growth rates are often in the far north, where the summer season is short, while the fastest are achieved in places which maintain year-round feeding temperatures. These include some spring-fed northern waters and mountain streams in equatorial regions.

The cooler oceans also offer excellent growing conditions, and most species are capable of visiting them. Salmon are genetically programmed to do so as are many stocks of trout and char; the only major species which appear incapable of entering salt water are the taimen and the North American lake trout. Prior to ocean migration most young salmonids lose their bright territorial colours and markings and acquire the silvery layer of guanine which marks their new status as smolts. Silvery flanks are typical of free-swimming shoal fish and this stage heralds a reversal of territorial behaviour; in the open sea they no longer need to compete for space but instead travel together in loose shoal formation. The smoltification process also involves physiological changes which prepare the young fish for entry into salt water. It occurs in spring or summer once the fish have reached a certain size and is followed by mass migrations seawards.

Growth rates in the sea can be spectacular especially among salmon. Feeding initially on small prey creatures, notably crustaceans such as shrimp, and later on fatty shoal fish, they commonly reach several pounds in weight in their first ocean year. Atlantic salmon may return to spawn after 18 months weighing 10–15 lbs and may gain 2 lbs a month during peak feeding periods. Trout and char normally feed closer to shorelines and grow more slowly although local races of steelhead and sea trout make longer migrations and may achieve equivalent growth rates to salmon. By the time they return to their parent streams mature salmon, trout and char will have built up sufficient fat reserves to last until spawning time as well as to develop reproductive organs.

Margin of lowland lake showing typical variety of aquatic plants. Most fish food is produced in shallow areas where light penetration is best.

Hardwood leaves. Leaf litter forms a base of the food chain in many streams: Hardwoods can also keep the water cool; the removal of tree cover, allowing stream temperatures to rise, is often cited as the main cause of the decline of the brook trout in its southern ranges. Conifers are of little benefit in food production. Their needles do not decompose easily but tend to clog spawning gravels and also acidify the water.

Reproduction

However distant their feeding grounds trout, salmon and char normally return to spawn in their parent water, often at the actual site where they themselves were born. Such places meet the prime requirements for successful reproduction – cold, clear, well-oxygenated water seeping through beds of stones or gravel. It is deep in these beds that their eggs will develop and the alevins find shelter in the first weeks after hatching. Fast, stony streams provide classic spawning water although char, and more rarely trout, may choose to spawn along the stony, wave-washed shores of lakes. The typical spawning period for rainbow and cutthroat trout is early spring, but most other species spawn in late autumn or winter.

The actual spawning procedure follows a similar pattern among all salmonids. The cock fish, attired in their distinctive breeding dress, normally arrive on the spawning ground ahead of the hens and engage in territorial displays, driving away other fish and competing with each other in ritual combat. The hens meanwhile wait until actual spawning time is close before moving in to excavate nests or redds. Before choosing a site a hen fish will check one or more spots by exploratory cutting of gravel. Having decided on a suitable place she will begin excavating; turning on her side and bending her body rapidly, her tail brushing above the stones, she uses the water pressure created by this action to shift them. Periodically she will stop and check the nest by lowering herself and exploring the bottom of it with her anal fin.

While the hen is engaged in cutting a cock fish will usually be in attandance. Other males may approach and he will turn on them with a dramatic display of flared fins and gaping mouth; if this fails to shift a rival he will chase it off. He may also turn on other species which gather at this time in expectation of a free meal of eggs, or on precocious male parr waiting to participate in the spawning act. The hen will also chase off any other females which attempt to encroach on her site.

Spawning Sequence (Atlantic salmon)

1. Hen fish exploring the site.

2. Cock fish chases intruders while hen cuts nest.

When the nest is ready she will settle into it and open her mouth just before starting to shed the first eggs. At this the cock moves in besider her and both fish quiver violently in orgasm as eggs and milt are ejected simultaneously. Precocious parr, lying unseen beneath the adult pair, sometimes succeed in shedding milt at the same time and, although an adult hen will not proceed to spawn in company with parr, it has been established that in some cases male parr can successfully fertilise the eggs.

Head of male Atlantic salmon showing jaw enlargements developed prior to breeding. The ritual purpose of the jaws sometimes extends to real combat with a rival male.

Immediately spawning is over the hen buries the eggs by shifting stones from upstream back into the hollow. She will continue cutting at the same place until a second nest is formed beside the first and the whole spawning sequence is then repeated. The female may spend a number of days in completing several nests, each adjoining the last. Once the process is over the male fish may remain on guard at the site for days and sometimes weeks. Virtually all of the thousands of eggs which may be laid by one hen fish will normally be successfully fertilised and, protected by the gravel, will hatch out in a period of weeks or months, depending on water temperature.

Although the spawning behaviour of different species follows a similar pattern the fate of spawners can be very different. The reproductive cells of Pacific salmon all ripen together, meaning they can breed only once, and the completion of a single spawning spells the end of their lives. Spent cohos may linger on for a few weeks but no Pacific salmon live to return to the ocean. Most Atlantic salmon also die after a single spawning. Males suffer more than females from the stress involved and survivors, which normally amount to under ten per cent, are mostly females.

Post-spawning mortality can also be high among steelhead rainbow trout and some races of sea trout, particularly those which make long ocean migrations. Multiple spawning is common, however, among most sea trout populations, as it is among brown, rainbow and cutthroat trout resident in fresh water.

Chars suffer least from the rigours of breeding and mortality is low among lake trout, Arctic char, dolly varden or brook trout.

3. The spawning act.

4. Hen covering the nest.

Hazards

The greatest threats to salmonid stocks are posed by man. Fishing pressures, though often publicised, are not always the most significant. Most stocks can recover quickly from the effects of over-fishing but not from the massive changes in habitat which have taken place since the beginning of the industrial era. Thousands of rivers have been, and often still are, used as repositories for waste products toxic to fish in general and the pollution-sensitive salmonids in particular. Dams have resulted in the extermination of migratory stocks of trout and salmon, while water abstraction has led to further habitat losses. Drainage schemes have caused the silting of nursery streams or the decimation of eggs and fry by flash floods, while logging operations have left others clogged with timber debris. The restocking of rivers and lakes has in many cases only resulted in the degradation of hardy native stocks by genetically unsuitable hatchery strains.

Ongoing problems are the increasing incidence of water acidification and eutrophication, or over-enrichment by agricultural nitrates and phosphates or from organic waste. Eutrophication commonly results in algal blooms which use up oxygen and kill aquatic fauna including fish.

The acid rain problem is potentially the most serious long-term threat since its effects are concentrated in unspoilt areas which, since the demise of major river systems in industrial regions, constitute the major strongholds of most salmonids. These areas are especially prone to acidification since many are acidic in nature already and it may take a relatively modest increase to impoverish or destroy fish and wildlife populations.

The primary cause of acidification is sulphur dioxide and oxides of nitrogen emanating from the burning of fossil fuels, notably in power stations, the burning of petroleum in motor vehicles, and the smelting of non-ferrous metals. Deposited either as a dry deposition from the air or as a wet deposition via rain, snow or mist, the effects of sulphuric and nitric acids can be greatly increased – and in some cases may only become lethal to fish – in conjunction with local factors such as the acidifying effect of blanket conifer plantations or the mineral run-off from mining operations. Aluminium, dissolved from the ground by acids, affects fish eggs and when present above certain concentrations will prevent them from hatching. The acid tolerance levels for different species vary from a pH of 4.5 for brook trout to 5.5 for rainbow trout: very high levels of acidity will kill fish outright. Water acidification can be a permanent condition; the only direct cure – the massive and regular addition of lime – is too expensive to apply on more than a few selected waters.

The first sign of dangerous acid levels is usually an increase in the

Map of southern Norway showing areas seriously affected by acid rain from the industrial regions of Britain and continental Europe. In the black areas fish life is virtually extinct.

size of an area's resident fish due to a drop in numbers and a consequent increase in available food for the survivors. An insidious aspect of the process is that it can cause a general decline in water productivity affecting the numbers of fish, birds and other wildlife. Many waters suffer a spring flush of acid from melting snow which, though brief, can kill fish at the sensitive fry stage.

PREDATORS Salmonid fish face natural predation at every stage of their lives. Eggs and fry are commonly eaten by members of their own species or by other fish. They are also taken by insects such as dragonfly larvae as well as by birds including mergansers, goosanders, dippers or gulls. In fresh water larger individuals are commonly eaten by herons, mink or otters, and by predatory fish such as pike. In the sea salmonids are eaten by many fish species as well as by cormorants, seals, dolphins or killer wales.

Otters have big appetites but their hunting territories are so large that fish stocks are unlikely to be seriously affected. The eel is the favourite food of both otters and herons; is forms their staple diet wherever it occurs.

PARASITES Parasite infestations are common among salmonids. Most wild fish are host to a number of different parasites, mainly small organisms which require detailed examination to detect. As predators require healthy fish on which to prey, so many parasites require healthy individuals and their presence only rarely has a serious effect on life or growth. An alien form or parasite, however, may damage whole stocks. Baltic salmon smolts carry the tiny crustacean *Gyrodactylus salaris* and, while they are largely immune to its effects, the accidental introduction of this creature to Norwegian salmon rivers has resulted in catastrophic mortalities.

Pike are capable of serious damage on stillwater trout fisheries; large and long-lived, they concentrate on eating the better class of trout favoured by anglers.

DISEASE Disease organisms are widespread in natural waters but again they only rarely have a significant effect on wild stocks. Major losses of migratory fish occurred when the disease UDN (Ulcerative Dermal Necrosis) hit British salmon and sea trout rivers in the 1960s; the cause of this condition has still not been identified. The effects of disease are usually much greater on fish farms than on wild populations, since farmed trout and salmon are much more prone to infections as a direct result of stress caused by the unnaturally high densities in which they are kept.

The seal is the only non-human predator which regularly decimates stocks of adult salmon and other sea-run salmonids. Seals often gather in estuaries where major runs of fish congregate; they sometimes follow the runs many miles into fresh water and their predations, though they may not be critical to spawning escapements, can seriously affect the livelihood of fishermen and fish farmers as well as the sporting potential of rivers.

1 ATLANTIC SALMON

Salmo Salar

JUVENILE STAGES

1 Egg before hatching

2 Alevin   Newly hatched young with yolk sac.

3 Fry   One inch (2.5 cm) long, at emergence from gravel.

4 Parr   4–8 inches (10–20 cm) long, can be told apart from small brown trout by their small mouth (the upper jaw does not reach the rear of the eye), pointed head, long pectoral fin, narrow tailstalk and deeply forked, sharp-ended tail. Red spots are mostly concentrated along the lateral line as in trout but parr marks are more distinct; salmon parr normally have only 1 to 4 spots on gill cover. Trout have a blunter head and tail and less delicate overall appearance.

5 Smolt   Similar in shape to parr but with silvery coats, are present in rivers in spring and early summer.

RETURNING ADULTS Salmon newly arrived from the ocean have bright silver flanks and whitish anal fins. Many carry sea lice on the body.

6 Spring salmon   These are typically blue-backed and hard-bodied; early season fish may show little difference between sexes. They are sometimes confused with mended kelts (see page 11) or with large sea trout (see below).

7 Summer grilse   Averaging 4–7 lbs, these often have distinctly forked tails. Those returning in autumn are sometimes large enough to be mistaken for two-sea-winter salmon.

8 Summer salmon   Male showing early stages of snout and jaw changes.

9 Summer salmon   Female showing typical colouring after 10–15 days in river.

Note: Big sea trout can be distinguished from fresh-run salmon by their long upper jaw extending beyond the rear of the eye and by their square-cut tail. They have a thicker tail stalk which makes a poor hand grip and often have many dark spots below the lateral line, whereas salmon rarely have more than a few, close to the lateral line at the front end.

SCALE AND FINRAY COUNTS Dorsal fin has 10–12 separate rays; there are 10 to 15 (usually 11–13) scales counted diagonally forwards from the lateral line to adipose fin.

SALMON FLIES from left: Jock Scott (traditional); Miramichi Squirrel and Rat Face McDougall (Canadian wet and dry patterns); Garry Dog and Stoats Tail (hairwings); Willie Gunn and Red and Black (Tube flies).

PLATE I

	1
3	2
5	4
	6
	7
	8
	9

RIVER ADULTS

10 September cock salmon after 3–4 weeks in either fresh or tidal water. The spots are beginning to develop irregular light halos, especially on the gill covers, and rusty red spots are forming. The pelvic and anal fins are turning dark. Spring runners will be darker overall while fish fresh from the sea will be silver-flanked: by September, however, all male fish will have well-developed hooked jaws.

11 Hen salmon in spawing dress The skin of both sexes becomes thickened and the slime covering more pronounced; females do not develop the enlarged jaws of the males and their coloration is more sober, usually pearly grey and purple-blue, occasionally turning blackish as spawning time approaches.

12 Cock salmon in spawning dress The jaws, used for ritual combat at the spawning redds, are at maximum size; the biggest, oldest fish have the most pronounced hooks. The body colouring of spawning males varies; the flanks may be apricot-orange to deep copper or red, the backs yellow-green to brown, purple or black. Rusty brown or orange spots and streaks are evident, particularly on the lower flanks and gill covers.

13 Kelt After spawning the surviving males rapidly lose the hooked jaw and by spring mended kelts are often bright silver. They can usually be distinguished from fresh run salmon by their thin shape, distended vents and the presence of gill maggots. They are rarely present in rivers after April. Salmon which have failed to spawn and are still full of eggs are sometimes encountered in rivers in spring.

LANDLOCKED SALMON Adults in summer dress. Landlocks are physically similar to anadromous fish but geographic isolation has resulted in the development of local forms with small differences in appearance.

14 Saimaa salmon Cock fish from Lake Saimaa, Finland, with characteristic small number of spots. Landlocks from Scandinavian lakes reach large sizes; a dwarf form, the blege, is found in some Norwegian lakes and rivers.

15 Sebago salmon The common lake dwelling form from eastern North America is typically heavily spotted.

16 Ouananiche The common river-dwelling form on the north shore of the St. Lawrence is often small with yellow-tinged flanks and heavy spotting.

PLATE II

	10	
	11	
	12	
	13	
14		
		16
15		

Names

Salmon are commonly described by their seasonal forms — spring, summer and autumn salmon. The name grilse is used for fish which return after a single winter in the ocean. Local terms may be used to describe distinctive runs of salmon, e.g. greybacks for big back-end fish in Scotland. *Salmo salar* means 'the leaper from the sea'. In North America landlocked Atlantic salmon are known as Sebago salmon and as Ouananiche.

Distribution

Atlantic salmon enter rivers and streams on both sides of the Atlantic from New England north to Ungava Bay, Quebec, and from the White Sea region of the USSR south to Portugal. They are most abundant in eastern Canada, the British isles and Scandinavia. Some European and North American salmon stocks overlap during their feeding migrations in the ocean, notably off southern Greenland, while others remain closer to their parent countries. Landlocked salmon are found in parts of eastern North America, Scandinavia and the western USSR; naturalised populations exist in Argentina and New Zealand.

Size

Grilse commonly average around 5 lbs but those arriving in autumn may be much larger. Salmon have generally spent two winters at sea and average 6–20 lbs, in different parts of their range. The multi-sea-winter salmon characteristic of certain rivers commonly exceed 20 lbs and some waters regularly produce them in excess of 30 lbs. Fish over 50 lbs are rare but 100-pounders have been reported from both sides of the Atlantic. The rod-caught record of 79½ lbs came from the Tana river which forms the border between Norwegian and Finnish Lapland.

Exploitation

The Atlantic salmon has long been the basis of valuable food fishery. Originally caught by a wide array of small-scale methods, the bulk of the wild catch is now taken in estuary nets, in drift nets and on long lines. The annual North Atlantic catch, including grilse, averages around 10,000 tons or about three million fish averaging 7 or 8 lbs each.

The most prestigious of all sporting fish, the Atlantic salmon is taken on rod and line from almost every river in which it occurs. The great value of the rod fishing has led to increased conservation of the species for anglers. Angling accounts for up to half a million salmon annually.

Life Cycle

JUVENILE LIFE The eggs of the Atlantic salmon hatch in spring and when the alevins have exhausted their yolk sacs they emerge from the gravel as free-swimming fry. Forming loose shoals in relatively fast, shallow water they begin feeding on small items in the drift of the stream. They require expanding territories as they grow in size and within a few weeks the density-dependent mortality usual among salmonids is likely to reduce their numbers by over 90 per cent. By the parr stage, at the start of their second year, the survivors will commonly comprise under five per cent of the original brood and in the continuing competition the population may be halved annually.

Survival pyramid showing typical mortality at main life stages of Atlantic and Pacific salmon. From bottom: 5,000 eggs, 350 fry, 50 smolts, 5 ocean adults, 2 spawning adults.

At some stage during their parr life young salmon lose their bright territorial colours and assume the silvery coat of the smolt in advance of their journey to the ocean. This change occurs when they have reached a particular size, often around six inches (15 cm); in southern rivers it will be after one or two years but in Arctic regions, where growth is slow, it may take five or six years. On many rivers there is a tendency for a proportion of the parr to become dominant, grow faster and migrate sooner than the remainder of the population. The smolt run takes place during May or June in most parts of the salmon's range and involves a mass movement down to salt water. Apart from the normal predation by birds or other fish *en route* the smolts sometimes face more serious hazards; unseasonal floods can cause heavy mortality by pushing them out to sea before they have had time to adjust to the saline environment, or to the temperature difference between river and sea, while a regular threat is presented by the pollution affecting some estuaries.

Smolts commonly spend some time around the river mouths before moving away from the coasts. Little is known about this phase of their life although it appears that, as has been shown for some of the Pacific salmons, they will remain in food-rich areas close to their parent rivers until supplies become inadequate for their increasing needs.

OCEAN LIFE Until the early 1950s the Atlantic destinations of salmon were a complete mystery and much remains to be learned. Publicity given to the Greenland feeding ground in the 1960s, when its importance became generally known, led many to assume that the mystery had been solved. Great numbers of salmon, particularly big two- and three-sea-winter fish, visit Greenland waters, about 40 per cent of them being of North American origin and 60 per cent European. It later became apparent, however, that many salmon never go near Greenland. Later a second major feeding ground, located around the Faroes, proved to be an important focus for big

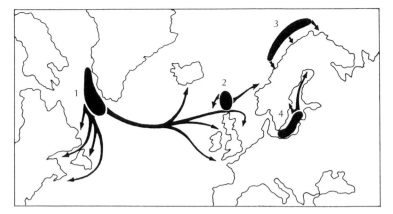

Major feeding grounds of Atlantic salmon. 1. SW Greenland 2. Faroes 3. Norwegian   4. Baltic

Norwegian salmon as well as for British grilse; a few North American salmon also travel as far as the Faroes.

Dramatic escalations in both the Greenland and Faroese fisheries led to fears for the survival of the species. Many salmon stocks, however, remained unaffected by either fishery. Many Norwegian fish feed off their own coasts in the Norwegian and Barents Seas, while Baltic salmon have been found to restrict their migrations to the southern Baltic Sea. Stocks from Canada's Big Salmon River were also found to feed close to home around the Bay of Fundy, thereby avoiding both the Greenland and Newfoundland fisheries. An unknown number of salmon also hunt beyond the reach of fishermen in the treacherous waters along the polar ice cap.

In all feeding grounds the food chain utilised by ocean-feeding salmon is based largely on crustaceans. They feed directly on nutritious shrimp and prawn as well as on fatty shoal fish such as sandeel, capelin, sprat and herring, which themselves rely on a crustacean diet. Commercial fisheries for these prey creatures, as well as natural fluctuations in their abundance, may influence both growth rate and feeding movements of salmon at sea.

The age at which they start back for their home waters is thought to be governed by hormonal changes associated with the onset of sexual maturity, with each river having characteristic proportions of grilse and older fish. Seasonal variations in these proportions as well as long-term trends, the so-called grilse and salmon cycles, may be influenced by environmental factors such as changes in ocean temperatures.

The means by which salmon find their way back to parent streams from hundreds or thousands of miles away remains unexplained. Theories include guidance by the earth's magnetic field, the stars or ocean currents. The first is based on the fact that salmon, like many other creatures including man, have a direction-finding mechanism based on an iron compound in the nasal area. It seems likely that this 'sixth sense' plays at least some part in guidance as has been proved among homing pigeons. Orientation by the stars has also been shown among some migratory birds and since salmon swim close to the surface celestial navigation is a possibility. So is a reaction to water movements; studies relating annual fluctuations in ocean currents to those of salmon migrations may indicate such a correlation. One navigational aid has been proved; once the fish reach coastal waters their sense of smell has been shown by experiment to guide them accurately to their parent stream and even to the pool of their birth.

RETURN TO THE RIVER Although salmon commonly enter big river systems in every month of the year, distinct runs occur at fairly set times in spring, summer or autumn. Their general timing is determined by genetic factors with the apparent aim of maximising the salmon's potential in a given river, with spring fish often sprawning in distant headwater streams and autumn runners in the lower reaches. The actual entry into fresh water is governed by local conditions. While rivers remain low the fish patrol nearby coasts or move in and out of estuaries with the tides. The reaction to a good rise in river level is immediate, with the whole group moving into fresh water; in a big, warm flood they often run hard upstream and in large rivers may cover more than 20 miles (32 km) in a single day. In cold water they travel more slowly. Grilse move up in groups while salmon tend to run in pairs, cock and hen together.

As the river level drops back the fish settle in sheltered holding pools where they may stay for months. Those entering in winter can spend up to a year in one stretch of river, living entirely off the fat reserves which, built up during their sea life, help to make the salmon such a desirable eating fish. During this time these considerable reserves are also used in the formation of eggs and milt.

With the onset of autumn floods the salmon will be on the move again. Their final run to the spawning grounds can be dramatic, the fish literally climbing mountains as they ascend headwater streams. The breeding sites or redds are located in shallow glides or the tails of pools; salmon make use of coarser sprawning gravels than trout and their redds include some fair-sized stones. The relative proportions of trout and salmon in a river system can be strongly influenced by the predominance of a particular size range in its spawning gravels.

November is the main spawning month on many rivers, and unlike Pacific salmons the Atlantic fish sometimes survives to spawn more than once. On Canada's Big Salmon River as many as eight sprawnings have been known but on most waters under ten per cent, mainly hen fish, do in fact recover. The weakened kelts or spent salmon succumb easily to disease although the ones which survive commonly regain the silvery appearance of fresh-run fish and are often mistaken for them when hooked by anglers after spring salmon. Kelts may be numerous in the lower reaches of rivers in March and April but by May most will have reached the ocean.

Atlantic salmon have been known to make straight leaps of at least 12 feet (3.5m) when surmounting waterfalls.

Angling

The capture of an Atlantic salmon on rod and line is often regarded as the ultimate angling achievement and huge amounts of time and money are spent in pursuance of it. It usually takes many days of fishing to land a first salmon yet thousands of fishermen persist. The first catch, however, may only be the start of an addictive experience, new horizons opening up with the possibility of better waters, more or bigger fish or the capture of the most desirable form of salmon, the fresh-run springer.

The Atlantic salmon's habit of showing itself can be very encouraging, especially for the beginner. The rivers often seem to be full of rolling and leaping fish. Experience soon shows, however, that their exuberance only too rarely extends to acceptance of the angler's offering.

The problem with adult salmon is that having acquired sufficient fat reserves in the ocean for their stay in fresh water they have little appetite for the river's pickings. Only very rarely has any item of freshwater food been found in their stomachs. Once in the river their stomachs apparently become incapable of digestion, and their occasional interest in the angler's lure will have little to do with actual feeding. Yet hundreds of thousands of salmon are taken on the rod every year, some by chance methods but most by techniques which have proved themselves over time.

Down-and-across is the standard tactic, whether it is fly, bait or spinner on the end of the line. The principle is to let the offering be taken round with the current so that it swings across in front of the spot where a salmon is judged to be lying. Fresh-run fish, particularly grilse, will sometimes head for the lure from a good distance away, but often it is necessary to bring it across the nose of a fish before it may be tempted to strike at it. Unlike trout, salmon are not easily put down by continuous casting and may eventually take after hours of repetitive effort; they can also respond positively to a change in the type or size of lure.

SPRING SALMON The classic qualities of the Atlantic salmon are epitomised by the fresh-run springer. Silver-sided, blue-backed and perfectly proportioned, it is the object of special devotion by the dedicated anglers who seek to catch it in the icy waters of late winter and early spring.

A knowledge of the river is especially important in spring fishing since these early salmon rarely show themselves in the manner of summer or autumn fish and must often be sought in known lies. In the cold waters of February and March they remain deep and, lacking the vigour which comes with higher temperatures, fresh-run fish tend to stay in the lower reaches of rivers below falls or other obstacles. Though less active than salmon at later seasons early

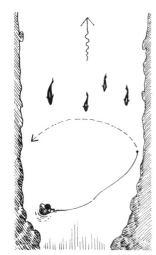

Down-and-across: the standard salmon fishing tactic for all methods.

springers are usually reckoned to be easier to catch, an important incentive considering their often small numbers.

Big artificial lures are standard for spring salmon fishing. Tobies or similar spoons are popular while the traditional and proven killer, the wooden yellow-belly Devon, probably accounts for more European springers than any other lure. Natural baits tend to be less effective in the early season than later on but big artificial flies fished on sinking lines are sometimes successful. As in all cold-water fishing it is vital that the lure be fished slowly and as close to the river bed as possible. The prime fighting condition and often large size of spring salmon may demand relatively strong tackle especially as river temperatures rise and they become more active.

Like summer steelhead the spring salmon has become relatively scarce in recent years while later runs have increased. A similar trend occurred in the late nineteenth century while in the middle years of the twentieth century spring fish often predominated. Today spring runs have virtually disappeared on many of the rivers which were once famous for them.

SUMMER SALMON AND GRILSE The start of the summer runs is often dramatic. It commonly coincides with high tides and summer rains, and the lack of new fish on some rivers in April or May is quickly remedied by the arrival of large numbers of fresh fish. For the first few days they are relatively easy to catch on bait, fly or spinner but as water levels drop back they settle into their chosen lies and become increasingly hard to tempt. It is then that the faster streamy parts of the river fish best and the classic summer technique of fly fishing with a floating line comes into its own.

Fly fishing is commonly regarded as the most pleasurable way of taking a salmon. While it has little of the scope or delicacy associated with trout fishing the salmon has an added liveliness when lightly hooked on fly. Small patterns fished quite fast and high in the water are favourites for low-water work in summer with morning and evening, and particularly the dusk spell, being the likeliest taking times. In low water salmon may take the dry fly, a method which is popular on Canadian rivers.

The large and decorative traditional salmon fly has been replaced by simpler patterns in a wide variety of sizes.

On many waters the summer run is dominated by large numbers of grilse. Energetic and often free-taking, these smaller salmon can provide excellent sport. They commonly arrive in the pools in large groups and while water levels remain high catches of several fresh-run fish a day are not exceptional. The earliest runs usually consist of individuals weighing from 4 to 6 lbs but as the season progresses the average size of new arrivals increases; by late autumn grilse often enter big rivers at double-figure weights.

AUTUMN SALMON In some areas autumn represents the peak of the fishing season. Many rivers have major runs at this time and in

Typical stances of hooked salmon. Head-shaking leaps are uncommon. Fish hooked in big pools usually stay in them; when they do not, the angler on foot may need to move fast to keep up with their powerful runs.

Common ways of baiting with worm (top) and shrimp or prawn. The latter are mostly used salted; they have a straightening pin through the centre and thread or light wire wound round the body. Natural baits can be fished on fly tackle as well as baitcasting gear.

some, such as those of southern Scotland, fresh-run fish can be caught up to the end of November. In addition the early season fish which have been holed up in big pools now take advantage of the autumn floods to move up towards the spawning grounds. These coloured fish, most of them impossible to tempt from their summer lairs, now once again offer the possibility of sport, while on the many small coastal streams, which lack early runs, the period after August may see the only action of the season.

Big spoons, spinners or flies are all popular for high-water fishing. Natural baits, however, are often reckoned to have the edge in attracting both summer and autumn fish, the most popular being worm, shrimp and prawn. The latter are particularly effective in low water and their smell seems to evoke in salmon memories of their ocean feeding days. The prawn can be an especially good taker but its odour is believed to unsettle other salmon in the vicinity for a considerable time and its use is banned on many waters. The popular worm has no such drawback. Three or four of the large garden variety bunched on a big single hook can be very effective either freelined or, in heavier currents, weighted to roll along the river bed. Salmon often take the worms gently and seem to enjoy chewing them, frequently taking the bait well down. A secure hookhold is likely provided the hook is not set until the salmon moves off of its own accord. When the bait is taken opposite or downstream of the angler he should if possible get below the fish so that the hook will find an optimum hold when it moves off, as it normally does, upstream.

Whatever bait is being used a critical moment is when, often after hours of repetitive effort, a fish is finally hooked. The beginner may think he has become snagged on the proverbial log, for unlike trout a salmon does not react quickly and it may be some time before it

18

realises anything is amiss. Many are lost when the 'log' unexpectedly moves off at high speed. If the angler is prepared for the fish with rod held high and the tackle in order he stands a better than even chance of landing it providing the hookhold is secure. The fight of the Atlantic salmon is less active than that of a trout, his runs powerful but steady and his leaps stately rather than acrobatic. Unlike trout, a salmon will often spend time trying to rid itself of the hook on the river bed – a dangerous manoeuvre wherever tree roots or other snags are present. It is the final stages of the fight which can be the most telling; salmon have great stamina and although they may allow themselves to be slowly drawn in will often continue to thrash at the surface or circle about at close range without lying on their side in the manner of a beaten fish. Too much pressure at the moment of landing can result in the hook pulling free or the line breaking.

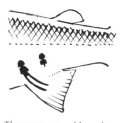

The presence of female sea lice with egg-laden 'tails' indicates a salmon fresh from salt water. Once the eggs drop off, the sea lice may still remain attached to the fish for several days.

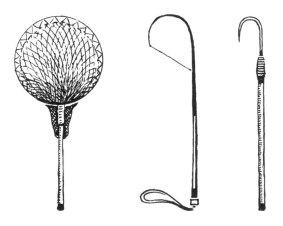

Landing net, tailer and gaff.

Many experienced fishermen prefer to land a salmon by tailing or by beaching it. If the fish can be drawn in steadily towards a gentle incline its own swimming movements will take it ashore; at this point it can be gripped firmly around the tail stalk and pushed a safe distance away from the water. Where the nature of the bankside prevents beaching a landing instrument such as a gaff, tailer or large landing net is needed. The gaff is commonly reckoned to be the most efficient tool for the job particularly when a salmon has to be lifted from fast, deep water up a steep bank. Landing nets are effective provided they are big enough – many salmon are lost in attempts to land them in trout-sized nets.

Salmon farm cage layout.

Salmon Farming

The practice of rearing Atlantic salmon in sea cages was pioneered in Norway in the 1970s and by the late 1980s the production from salmon farms exceeded by many times that of the commercial fisheries. Norwegian production increased from 1,000 tons a year in 1975 to 27,000 tons in 1985. Meanwhile the Scottish industry had also got under way and by 1987 production there had reached 15,000 tons. Large-scale farms have now been established in several countries and the total output is so large that the Atlantic salmon is once again becoming the widely available eating fish it was in the past. A significant side-effect of the price stabilisation has been the reduced viability of commercial fishing for wild salmon and the possibilities for conserving more wild stocks for rod fishing.

Salmon Ranching

The practice of ranching was developed in Japan where an important industry has been established based on the Pacific chum salmon. Atlantic salmon ranching is essentially different in that its young need to be raised for a year in fresh water before being released into the ocean. Naturally imprinted with the memory of the water in which they were raised, between four and ten per cent of them can be expected to return over a period of from one to three years. Though still a small industry compared to farming, salmon ranching operations are established in a number of countries, most notably Iceland.

Commercial Fishing

Once the subject of a wide array of small-scale fishing methods, wild Atlantic salmon are now mainly taken by long lines, draught nets, stake nets and drift nets. Long lines comprise baited hooks set at intervals on a main line up to several miles in length. Employed on the salmon's ocean feeding grounds, its main use is off Greenland, Norway, in the Baltic and off the Faroes, where it is the principal means of capture. Draught nets (or net and coble) are used by small boats to encircle groups of salmon in estuaries while stake nets comprise a wall of netting, fixed at one end to the shore, which deflects salmon towards a trap at the other end. Drift netting commonly involves the setting of miles of gill nets on ocean feeding grounds, or across migration routes to intercept salmon returning to the coasts. With the introduction of nylon monofilament, which is practically invisible to the fish, this method became so deadly that many countries have banned its use. It is also believed to leave many salmon fatally injured and most drift net fisheries are under pressure to cease operations from bodies concerned with the management of salmon.

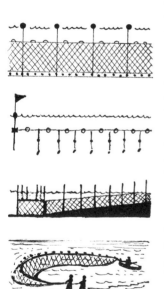

Main commercial methods from top: drift net, long line, stake net, draught net.

Landlocked Salmon

Natural populations of landlocked Atlantic salmon are found on both sides of the Atlantic but it is in the north-eastern US, where most anadromous stocks have been lost, that it is of particular importance. Named after lake Sebago in Maine where it was first recognised and studied, the range of the Sebago salmon has been extended to many deep lakes throughout New England and in New York State, together with the smelt, the forage fish on which it largely relies for its adult growth. East Canada has a widely distributed river-dwelling form, the Ouananiche.

Sebago Salmon spawn in autumn in either the inlet or outlet streams of lakes. Their growth rates vary but are slower than those of sea-run salmon; rod-caught fish commonly average 1 – 4 lbs and rarely exceed 10 lbs. In appearance they are similar to anadromous fish apart from their generally heavier spotting.

Famous for its frequent high leaps when hooked, the landlock is reckoned to be a particularly good fighting fish, perhaps because it is normally taken during its active feeding phase rather than on its spawning migration. At ice-out times it is often taken on streamer flies or spoons worked near the surface, but when the upper layers of the lakes heat up salmon seek the cooler depths and are mainly sought by trolling with fly or spoon, or with natural baits. Each area has its favourite fly patterns for landlock fishing but most are designed as imitations of forage fish, notably smelt. Small dry flies will also take them during the evening when they come up to feed near the surface.

The Ouananiche has a more varied distribution than the Sebago form, occuring naturally in a number of rivers on the north shore of the St Lawrence. In some areas it rarely exceeds 1 or 2 lbs.

European landlocks vary in size from the dwarf forms found in a few Norwegian waters to the big fish of lakes in Sweden, Finland and the USSR. Those in southern Sweden, notably Lake Vanern, have growth rates similar to anadromous salmon, as do those of Lake Saimaa in Finland and Lake Ladoga in the western USSR. In these large waters landlocks commonly average over 5 lbs with occasional specimens of 15 – 20 lbs.

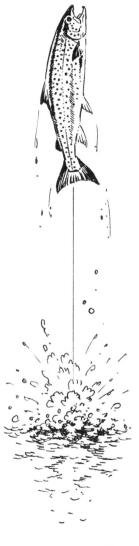

Status

In spite of the oft-expressed fears for its survival the overall status of the Atlantic salmon has remained generally stable in recent years. Nevertheless few rivers achieve their full potential in terms of the numbers or size range of salmon they produce and many continue to suffer setbacks as a result of habitat losses or heavy commercial exploitation. The greatest blow to the species occurred in the late nineteenth and early twentieth centuries with the loss of major rivers in the southern parts of its range. The Rhine, once reckoned the world's greatest salmon river, was reduced to the chemical sewer it remains today while the Seine, the Thames, the Elbe and other major European rivers were similarly rendered unfit for the passage of salmon. In North America most US stocks were wiped out with the loss of the Connecticut and all but a few small New England streams.

In its northern strongholds the salmon, though often under heavy fishing pressure, remains a common fish. On the Atlantic seaboard of Canada most rivers have substantial runs as do those of Scotland, Ireland, Iceland and Norway, while in northern or temperate regions of several other countries it remains locally abundant. The bulk of the rod catch is shared in approximately equal proportions between Canada, the British Isles and Scandinavia.

CANADA The Maritime Provinces are renowned for their wealth of unspoilt fly-only salmon rivers. The best known is probably New Brunswick's Miramichi which accounts for most of the province's rod catch; it commonly produces over 20,000 fish a year, mainly grilse but with a proportion of larger fish. Nova Scotia has over thirty rivers and streams including the St Mary's, the Grand, the La Have, the Medway, the Moser and the Margaree. As elsewhere in Canada most are summer rivers but the Margaree is known for its late run of relatively large salmon. Newfoundland has a wealth of grilse-producing rivers with some of the wilderness waters of Labrador noted for larger salmon as well; the total rod catch is usually around 30,000 fish. Quebec has some important southern rivers, including the well-known Matapedia, the Restigouche and the Moise, as well as the George and other subarctic waters of the Ungava Bay region.

In recent years cutbacks on commercial fishing have enhanced stocks in many Canadian rivers. Strict angling regulations apply everywhere, with fly-only being the almost universal rule. Most Quebec and New Brunswick rivers are privately owned or leased to outfitters; those of Nova Scotia and Newfoundland are public waters.

US In New England major restoration programmes are under way to return the Connecticut, the Merrimack, the Penobscot and other formerly important salmon rivers to their original state. In 1987 seven streams in Maine had small self-sustaining salmon runs.

SCOTLAND In addition to its historic importance in the development of salmon angling Scotland is a major producer nation with declared rod catches averaging some 70,000 fish a year. The major east-coast rivers such as the Spey, the Dee, the Tay and the Tweed are the best known; the Tay rod catch is commonly around 15,000 salmon averaging over 10 lbs. The west coast has over 200 smaller streams and rivers, producing mainly grilse and small salmon, in addition to the larger south-western rivers, such as the Nith and the Annan. The best spring runs are mainly found in north-eastern rivers; most waters have good summer runs while the larger southern rivers are noted for very late ones.

The angling potential of many important Scottish rivers has increased in recent years with netting rights having been bought out by sporting and conservation groups. The Clyde, the only notable river to have lost its salmon run, is the subject of a major restoration programme. No rod licence is required in Scotland but most salmon fishing is privately owned; the top beats are expensive but cheap fishing can be had on numerous association and hotel waters. Angling restrictions vary; a fly-only rule is common during low-water conditions.

ENGLAND & WALES The most important salmon rivers in England are the Wye, which commonly produces around 4,000 rod-caught salmon averaging 12 lbs; the Hampshire Avon, which has a small run of big spring fish averaging 25–30 lbs; and several northern waters including the Lune, the Eden, the Tyne and the Wear. The two biggest English rivers – the Thames and the Trent – are the subject of restoration programmes. Welsh rivers are dominated by sea trout but most have salmon runs as well; the Teifi, the Towy, the Conway, the Dee and the upper Wye can all be productive.

IRELAND Most major salmon rivers are found on the east coast and include the Blackwater, the Suir, the Nore, the Slaney and the Boyne. These are best known for their spring and summer runs. West coast waters include the Shannon and the Ballynahinch fishery in addition to many small streams with summer and autumn runs. Some Irish rivers have declined in recent years but in spite of periodic commercial over-fishing most maintain fair and sometimes good runs of fish.

ICELAND Iceland enjoys a unique reputation for unspoilt salmon rivers. The first country to phase out commercial fishing in favour of angling, its 80 rivers produce over 40,000 salmon a year. Most are in the western half of the country; those with catches normally exceeding 2,000 fish a year include the Laxa in Adaldur, the Thvera and the Midfjardara. The Laxa in Adaldur has the highest average size at 12½ lbs; the average on other rivers is between 6 and 8 lbs.

Strict protection measures have ensured the continued high productivity of rivers; Icelandic salmon fishing is not cheap but the high catch returns make it a favourite for visiting anglers.

NORWAY Famed for the large size of its salmon, Norway also has more major rivers than any other country. Here even small rivers produce large salmon and on big waters such as the Laerdal, the Vosso, the Tana and the Alta they commonly average over 20 lbs. Salmon rivers are spread throughout the length of the country including the subarctic regions; the famous Alta, often regarded as the world's best salmon river, as well as the record-producing Tana are both in the north. On most Norwegian waters the larger salmon enter from mid-June to mid-July with the later part of the season dominated by grilse runs.

Increased restrictions on commercial fishing, including the phasing out of drift-net fishing, are leading to enhancement of river stocks. However, over 30 rivers and streams including the famous Driva have lost virtually their entire salmon stocks since the accidental introduction of the Baltic salmon parasite *Gyrodactylus salaris* which kills salmon at the smolt stage. Acid rain has also ruined several rivers in the south of the country.

Most Norwegian rivers are leased by fishing associations which issue permits. As elsewhere, the top waters are expensive.

FINLAND The best-known salmon river in Finland is the Tenojoki which forms the border between Finnish and Norwegian Lapland and is known in Norway as the Tana. The Teno regularly produces fish of 20–40 lbs while the other northern salmon river, the Naatamojoki, is known for big catches of smaller salmon. July and August are the best fishing months.

SWEDEN Commercial pressures from several Baltic nations have long put pressure on Baltic salmon stocks and most rely heavily on hatchery fish. About 30 Swedish rivers have salmon runs but the only one of note is the Morrum which has a small run of big fish.

FRANCE Several rivers in Brittany have moderate salmon runs and there are a few self-sustaining rivers in the south. Major rivers such as the Seine and the Loire have long been lost but enhancement measures are leading to a gradual increase of stocks on others.

SPAIN There are several good salmon rivers running out of the Cordillera range in the northern Asturia area. The best include the Narcea, the Eo, the Ulla, the Mino, the Sella, the Deva-Cares and the Ason. Catches on most of these exceed 1,000 fish a year; the total rod catch is normally around 10,000. Salmon fishing in Spain is well regulated, easy to obtain and relatively inexpensive.

Conservation

The best-known member of the salmon family also provides a classic example of human mismanagement. For thousands of years it was an abundant fish and an integral part of economic and cultural life in the North Atlantic basin. Then, in the space of 50 years, this huge resource was hit by the destruction of major rivers throughout the southern parts of the salmon's range. The costly and painstakingly slow rehabilitation of waters on both sides of the Atlantic has barely begun to rectify the damage; on its once-greatest river, the Rhine, the process has yet to start. Meanwhile in its northern ranges it has been the subject of bitter disputes between interested groups.

In 1956 the international controversy was heralded by the capture off Greenland of a tagged Scottish salmon, followed by more from other European countries and Canada. It soon became evident that a major feeding ground had been discovered and for the first time the salmon, which until then had been managed almost exclusively by producer nations, became vulnerable to uncontrolled ocean fishing. By 1966 several European nations had established a major offshore fishery which included the use of the new and deadly monofilament drift net. During the same decade the discovery of the Faroes feeding ground led to the creation of a major long-line fishery as well as contentious new drift-net operations off Canada, Norway, Ireland, Scotland and England. The Atlantic salmon resource had become in urgent need of management at international level.

The most efficient way of managing salmon stocks is by harvesting them as they return, at full adult size, at the approaches to their parent rivers. Unlike the Pacific species, however, Atlantic salmon management is complicated by the fact that many stocks feed in the territorial waters of non-producer nations and, if they are to be harvested commercially at all, a part of the catch can fairly be demanded by such countries as a 'grazing fee'. The 1970s saw a long process of international wrangling and complex negotiations which, while still continuing, has already done much, by way of quotas and limitations on catching methods, to reduce the excesses of the free-for-all which followed the finding of the ocean feeding grounds.

For salmon anglers the situation has also been slowly improving. An increased awareness of the value of rod fisheries, as well as the need to ensure good spawning escapements, has encouraged governments to further limit commercial fishing. At the same time the rapid increase in salmon farming has caused an effective fall in market prices and resulted in incentives for government or sporting interests to buy out coastal nets. Future moves in salmon conservation may turn increasingly towards restoration of rivers and efforts to combat the increasing incidence of water acidification.

Releasing salmon. Fresh run fish are best killed since they are unlikely to escape infection and death from small skin abrasions received during the fight. Once in fresh water they gradually acquire tougher skins, but should always be released without handling.

2 PACIFIC SALMONS

FRY AND OCEAN ADULTS

1 Pink Salmon   Ocean adults can be distinguished from other species by the very large spots on body and tail (the largest at least eye-sized), by the very small scales, and by the distinctive pink flesh. Fry are recognized by their lack of body markings; they are present in rivers for only a short period in spring.

2 Sockeye Salmon   These can be told apart from all other species except chum by their very small speckles, from chum by a gillraker count in excess of 25. Kokanee or lake-dwelling sockeye (left) are silver-sided, green-backed and usually under 12 inches (30 cm) long. Sockeye fry are distinguishable by their light markings, mostly above the lateral line; they move into lakes soon after emerging.

3 Chum Salmon   Ocean adults can be differentiated from the similar sockeye by a gillraker count below 25, and occasionally by the presence of faint, gridlike bars on the body. They also have a characteristic head shape and dark tips to pectoral and tail fins. Chum fry have similar markings to sockeye but are identifiable by their bright olive-green mottled backs: they migrate to sea soon after emergence.

4 Coho Salmon   Ocean adults have moderate sized spots on the body and the tail (normally on the upper lobe only). They are distinguished from the similar chinook by the white gumline. Fry and parr have prominent long, narrow parr marks and long leading edges to dorsal and anal fins; they may be found year-round in streams and rivers.

5 Chinook Salmon   Deeply built and with distinctly forked tails, chinook have moderate sized spots on body , dorsal fin and tail (usally both lobes). They are distinct from other species in their black gumline. Ocean adults commonly have brownish backs and a purplish flush on the flanks. Fry and parr have large oval parr marks; the anal fin is normally uncoloured with a short leading edge. They can be found in rivers through the summer months.

6 Masu   Found only off Asian coasts, ocean adults are typified by their very deep build and relatively small size. The landlocked amago form (left) is less silvery; it often retains parr marks, pinkish flanks and distinct spots. Fry and parr are variously coloured but have distinct blue parr marks with round spots below; this is the only Pacific salmon which may have red spots as well.

PLATE III

1
2
3
4
5
6

Pacific salmons can be distinguished from all other salmonids by their long anal fins with 13–19 rays.

BAITS   Spoon, plug, squid imitation, natural herring (for ocean trolling); spoon and fly (for river fishing).

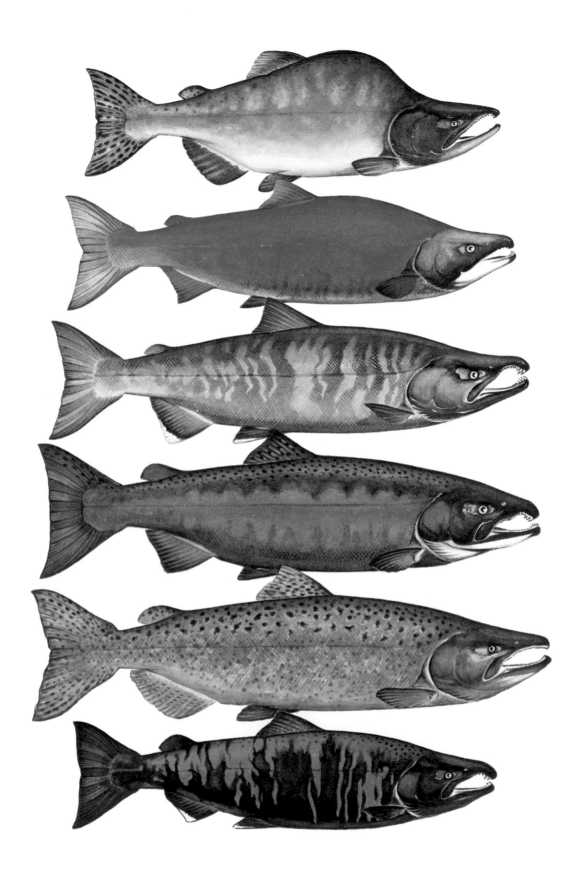

MALES IN BREEDING DRESS

1 Pink Salmon The huge, laterally flattened hump of the male is characteristic. The flanks are reddish to yellowish with dull vertical streaks. The jaws are elongated, the snout moderately hooked. Females lack the hump and enlarged jaws; they are typically olive-green on the flanks with slight streaks. The tails of both sexes retain the large, prominent spots characteristic of the species.

2 Sockeye Salmon Both sexes are distinguished from other species by the distinctive red-and-green colouration. Males develop a moderate hump and elongated jaws. The red on body and fins is brighter on fish which travel inland than those which spawn near the coast. The head is pale green with a dark upper jaw contrasting with the white lower one.

3 Chum Salmon The massively developed fangs are characteristic of spawning males. The flanks have distinct vertical streaks of black or reddish with dull green spaces between. Females lack the extreme jaw development and their coloration is muted. Both sexes have white tips to pectoral and anal fins.

4 Coho Salmon The males develop a distinct hook on the upper jaw; they are brick red to bright red on the flanks, greenish on the back and dark on the belly. Females are dull bronze and may have irregular reddish or purple patches on the flanks; they have a slight jaw enlargement.

5 Chinook Salmon Spawners lack the pronounced breeding dress of other species. Females become dark brown to black; the males have moderately enlarged jaws and dull yellow or reddish flanks. A distinctive feature is the spotting on body, dorsal fin and both lobes of the tail.

6 Masu Salmon Anadromous males have strongly hooked upper jaws and dark bodies with red vertical streaks. Females are pale yellow-green or brown with faint pinkish streaks on the flanks; they lack the hooked jaw. Both sexes have a white-tipped anal fin.

PLATE IV

| 1 |
| 2 |
| 3 |
| 4 |
| 5 |
| 6 |

COHO SALMON

Oncorhynchus kisutch

Names
The official name 'Coho' derives from Indian usage. Common names include silver salmon and, for young fish, blueback. The scientific term 'kisutch' is from the vernacular in Kamchatka. *Oncorhynchus*, the genus to which all Pacific species belong, means 'hook-nose'.

Distribution

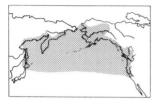

The coho enters small streams and rivers from Hokkaido north to the Anadyr river and from Point Hope, Alaska, south to Monterey Bay in California. Its main North American spawning range is from the Columbia river north to Cook Inlet, Alaska. In the ocean some stocks from both sides of the Pacfic may overlap during their feeding migrations.

Coho are sometimes stocked in fresh water and in the Great Lakes of eastern North America they have established a breeding population.

Size
After a year in the ocean young coho weigh 2–3 lbs but at full maturity, in the autumn of the same year, most weigh 4–12 lbs. Exceptionally they exceed 20 lbs and the ocean rod record, which came from Cowichan Bay, British Columbia, in 1947, weighed 31 lbs. In the Great Lakes introduced coho reach equivalent sizes and one of the 33 lbs was angled from Lake Michigan in 1970.

Exploitation
The coho is the mainstay of the Pacific salmon sport fishery. Famous for its active, leaping fight it is taken along the coastline from May to October and in rivers and streams in early autumn. An excellent eating fish, it is also a favoured species in traditional food fisheries where it is taken by small-scale methods including spear, gaff, net and fish weirs. As a commercial species the coho ranks fourth in overall importance after the sockeye, the pink and the chum; it is taken mainly by inshore trolling.

Commercial trolling for coho and chinook is a development of the 'poverty sticks' of the depressed 1930s. Four poles are usually used each carrying a heavy weight and several lures attached to droppers off a metal line. A bell at the top of each pole signals a strike. Seine and gill nets are also employed in the coho fishery and the catch is sold either fresh or frozen.

An important species for fish farming, the coho is widely reared in saltwater cages in North America and occasionally elsewhere.

Life cycle

Coho typically spend a year in fresh water after their spring emergence from the gravel except in northern areas where a two-year stay is more common. Favouring the slower-moving parts of rivers and streams, the fry and parr are highly territorial, their distinctive parr marks and strongly marked fins enhancing aggressive displays towards rivals. Prior to their springtime seaward migration they lose these markings and acquire the silvery dress of the smolt.

Lateral threat display of juvenile coho. Long parr marks are typical of species living in slow water; their display effect is enhanced by the stripes on raised dorsal and anal fins.

The first ocean year is spent in the surface layers of coastal waters feeding on small food items including small crustacea, young fish and wind-or current-borne terrestrial insects. By the following spring they will have reached 2lbs or more and their diet will increasingly consist of oily shoal fish such as sand lance and small herring. At this time many coho begin moving into deeper water and some will travel up to a thousand miles into the ocean. By late summer the maturing fish will be moving back towards their home rivers, feeding as they go. The voracious appetite of these fish during their final months at sea results in their reaching an average weight of around 8 lbs by the time they enter fresh water.

In the far north coho begin entering the rivers in June and July but in the southern regions the main runs will be from late August to October. Although a few small precocious males or jacks return after their first summer at sea the great bulk of the fish consist of individuals which have spent some 18 months there. At this stage they are nearing the end of their third year or, in the case of those which spent two years in fresh water as juveniles, their fourth.

Coho favour small waters in which to spawn and will enter tiny coastal creeks as well as river tributaries. Once in fresh water their bright blue-and-silver ocean dress is quickly replaced by spawning colours including greenish-blue back, dark belly and bronze or reddish flanks. The flanks of the male often turn crimson and the snout becomes black, elongated and hooked. The spawning sequence follows the usual salmonid pattern, a female digging a series of nests and mating in each with a dominant male while smaller males, including jacks, dash in to shed milt at the same time. Unlike other Pacific salmons coho often linger on through the winter before dying.

Spawning coho. The hooked snout of the male is typical of Pacific salmons.

Original Indian trolling gear. Abalone shell lure with hair leader and hardwood hook (top) and bone-tipped hook for fishing natural herring strip. Stone sinker above leader allowed bait to be fished at required depth.

Angling

Ocean angling starts in april or May, when the young 'blueback' coho are reaching a catchable size of over 2 lbs and continues on through the summer, reaching a peak in August when the offshore shoals return to the coasts. Estuary and river fishing is carried out from late summer into autumn.

Saltwater methods include trolling, mooching and bucktailing. In estuaries and rivers coho are taken on bait, spinner and fly.

Salmon trolling has been a part of life on the Pacific coast for thousands of years. Indian fishermen used abalone shell lures and knotted kelp lines with braided hair leaders as one of the diverse methods used to take the fish on which the economy of the coastal peoples depended. New settlers learend the practice, introducing steel hooks and gut lines to a technique which remains essentially the same among today's sport fishermen. Success depends on a knowledge of seasonal locales and a subtle arrangement of terminal tackle, varied to suit the mood of the fish, as well as on a readiness to alter fishing depth and speed according to tidal and diurnal movements of the bait fish shoals which herald the presence of salmon.

A more recent addition to basic trolling gear is the herring dodger or flasher. Attached between hook and weight, it attracts salmon from a distance and imparts an attractive movement to the bait. Effective trolling speeds vary from two to four knots; too slow a speed tends to attract dogfish while too fast a pace will twist the line and interfere with the steady action of the dodger.

Coho usually hunt in the upper water layers and can be searched from from the surface down to 100–130 ft (30–40 metres). Ideally the herring shoals which form a staple part of the salmon's diet should be located first. They can often be spotted dimpling at the surface or their presence is indicated by a concentration of gulls. Simple echo-sounders are a common mechanical aid not only in locating herring shoals but in following the contours of the sea bed; it can pay to fish around the underwater reefs and spurs around which the shoals congregate. Salmon are often found alongside the tide-rips off headlands, hunting the feed swept by in the current or sheltering in the eddies.

The diurnal movements of herring are particularly important to salmon movements. At night vast quantities of euphausiid shrimps rise to the surface attended by the herring shoals which prey on them. At dusk and dawn coho salmon can often be seen, and caught, as they hunt the herring.

When trolling for coho it is not unusual to hook chinook salmon, particularly when fishing deep, and the same basic method can be used for both species. Mooching, described on page 34, is another

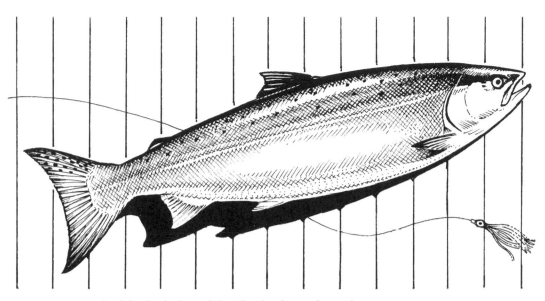

Ocean-caught coho.

important method for both these fish. The third popular technique, bucktailing or flashtailing, is used exclusively for coho.

BUCKTAILING The attraction of bucktailing lies in the light gear fished on or near the surface for the well-grown coho of late summer and early autumn. It is a particularly successful method in areas like the east coast of Vancouver Island where shoals of big fish concentrate *en route* to their home streams. It combines trolling with fly fishing, and the big double-hooked hairwing fly is arranged so that it skips along in the propellor wash 50–65 ft (15–20 metres) astern of the boat. The coho strike hard and hook themselves and since little or no weight is used on the line they are free to give their best fighting performance. The fight of the coho can rival that of any salmonid fish with its powerful runs and frequent leaps.

Hairwing flies can also be used on standard fly tackle from a drifting or stationary boat. Spinning or strip casting with herring bait can also be employed. While these methods are not effective in locating salmon they can be used successfully where concentrations of coho have been spotted at the surface.

Freshwater gear can be used to take coho in estuaries and rivers as the shoals return to fresh water. Bucktail and streamer flies, fished near the surface, are often successful in tempting coho around river mouths while bar fishing with a bottom rig baited with salmon eggs is a popular method in the lower reaches of big rivers.

Once in fresh water coho, like all Pacific salmons, remain in good condition for a relatively short time. While they are still fresh-run they can give good sport on fly, spinner or bait but their willingness to take the angler's offering varies and while they are popular quarry on some rivers, on others they are little sought after. Their fighting qualities and edibility remain good for two or three weeks after their entry into fresh water.

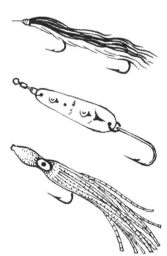

Standard artificials for coho include bucktail fly (top), Tom Mack spoon and the Hoochie, a plastic squid imitation popular with sport and commercial trollers on both sides of the Pacific.

CHINOOK SALMON

Onocorhynchus tshawytscha

Names

the official name chinook derives from an Indian band on the lower Columbia, the most renowned chinook salmon river. In California it is commonly called the king salmon, in British Columbia the spring salmon and fish over 30 lb are often referred to as tyee, an Indian name meaning 'chief'. The New Zealand name quinnat derives from the Alaskan name and the scientific name 'tshawytscha' comes from the vernacular in Kamchatka.

Distribution

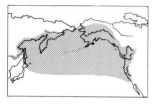

Chinook salmon enter the larger rivers from Hokkaido north to the Anadyr river and from Point Hope, Alaska, down to the Ventura river in southern California. Ocean-feeding fish of both Asian and North American origin may meet in the north-central Pacific Ocean.

The chinook has sometimes been stocked outside its native range, mainly for angling purposes. It is now an important sport fish in the Great Lakes and in the South Island of New Zealand self-sustaining populations of both sea-run and lake-dwelling chinook have been established.

Size

The largest of all salmon, mature chinook generally average 15–20 lbs. Most inshore-caught fish are between 5 and 10 lbs but weights of 20–60 lbs are not uncommon in favoured locations. Angling records include river-caught fish of 93 lbs from Alaska and 92 lbs from British Columbia. Commercially caught chinook of around 100 lbs have been reported many times; the largest authenticated was caught in a trap in Alaska and weighed 126 lb 3oz.

Exploitation

As a sporting fish the chinook is a near rival in popularity to the coho. Though less acrobatic when hooked, it grows much larger and unlike the coho it can be caught in the ocean through the winter months. Although neither chinook nor coho have naturally occuring freshwater populations their successful introduction in the Great Lakes and elsewhere has proved their potential for planting in suitable waters outside their natural range.

The chinook is the most important species for the fresh food market. In California it is the principal commercial salmon although in overall commercial importance it is the least valuable of the five main species. In North America most chinook are taken by trolling. For Pacific fish farmers the chinook, like the coho, is a favoured species.

Life Cycle

Chinook fry emerge from the gravel in spring and after a brief schooling period take up individual territories. They are not as aggressively territorial as coho fry and typically spend less time in the rivers before migrating seaward. Most leave within a few months although in northern regions they may spend one to two years in fresh water.

On arrival in the ocean young chinook at first remain near the coast, feeding at a greater depth than young coho but on a similar diet of easily available small creatures. Later they begin their ocean travels, feeding on oily shoal fish such as herring, sand lance and pilchard and making long journeys both along the coasts and out into the central Pacific. A minority return to the rivers as jacks of 2 or 3 lbs, but most chinook remain at sea from three to five years, and occasionally as long as eight, attaining weights of 15 lbs and more.

Sand lance or sand eel, a staple for anadromous salmonids in both Pacific and Atlantic inshore waters.

While other Pacific salmon return to fresh water in late summer or autumn chinook may have spring, autumn and winter runs in the same river. Spring runs tend to be small, the fish moving well upstream to await the autumn spawning period, while autumn runners often spawn in the lower reaches. Although chinook do sometimes enter small streams to spawn, their typical spawning areas are in relatively deep water over heavy gravels in fairly large rivers. The best-known chinook rivers are the largest entering the north Pacific. In California the chinook fishery relies heavily on the Sacramento-San Joaquin system, in Oregon and Washington the Columbia, in British Columbia the Fraser and in Alaska the Yukon. On the Asian shore the big Amu and Anadyr Rivers are the most important. Numerous other rivers of moderate size have good chinook runs but, unlike the big rivers, these are often restricted to autumn.

The spawning dress is less exotic than that of other Pacific salmons. The hen fish turns a dark, drab shade overall while the flanks of the males become dull yellow or reddish and its jaws become only slightly enlarged.

The chinook has a preference for deep-water habitats at every stage. Its fry and parr tend towards the deeper stretches of rivers while in the ocean most hunting takes place at depths below those favoured by other species. Such habitat specialisation is found among all the Pacific salmons and accounts for a broader use of the environment – and a larger total mass of fish – than would be possible for a single, less specialised species.

Chinook post-smolt. The pelagic lifestyle is emphasized by the powerful, streamlined body shape and crescent-like tail.

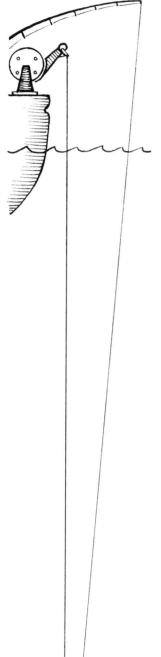

Angling

Chinook are sought on rod and line from the same inshore areas as coho and the main methods – trolling, described on page 30, and mooching – apply to both. The main difference in fishing tactics centres on the chinook's habit of feeding deep and a bait fished close to the sea bed is often most effective. The lures and herring baits used for coho are also employed for chinook although larger artificials including big plugs are sometimes favoured.

The downrigger is a popular addition for trolling at depths below the reach of normal gear. A sinker of 5–20 lbs is attached to a stainless steel wire with the main line attached by a quick release clip above the lead. A downrigger with line-counter allows the bait to be fished at a specific depth and when used in combination with an echo-sounder can make for accurate coverage of different water levels while reducing the risk of snagging the bottom. The downrigger method also allows a better play from the fish since there is no lead on the main line to impede its movements.

Mooching, which is commonly reckoned a more interesting style of fishing then trolling, is practised either from a drifting boat or a craft at anchor. It involves the use of a 9–12 ft (2½–3½ metre) through-action rod, a centrepin reel loaded with 15–20 lb line, a small lead and herring bait. Two such outfits may be used, one weighted with an ounce or so of lead and fished at around 65 ft (20 metres) depth for coho, the other weighted with two or three ounces and fished above the sea bed for chinook. The precise amount of lead can be varied according to current speed; in order to avoid the bait wrapping round the line as it sinks the gear is cast well clear of a static boat. When using herring plug or strip the hooks should ideally be attached so that the bait revolves slowly when retrieved and if a fish is contacted the gear can be fished at that depth on the next cast.

Salmon have a habit of playing with a herring and the timing of the strike can be crucial. Chinook often swim upwards with a deeply fished bait, resulting in the line angling away from the rod tip, and fast retrieve is then necessary before the hook can be set. It is not advisable to fish immediately above the sea bed since various species of ground fish find a slowly revolving herring very attractive.

Although daytime fishing means well-sunk baits dawn and dusk provide opportunities to take chinook near the surface. At these times they often move into the upper water layers to feed, as do other salmonids in both salt and freshwater environments. During summer chinook can sometimes be seen porpoising in the calm waters of shallow bays and inlets but catching them at these times is notoriously difficult.

The long ocean life of the chinook means that it provides

Downrigger trolling.

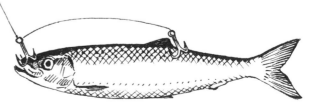

year-round fishing. While the average weight of ocean-caught fish is under 10 lbs much bigger ones are always possible and there are certain well-known areas, notably narrows, inlets and estuaries, where in summer and autumn outsize fish can be expected. In places such as Discovery Passage in British Columbia hotels, lodges and fishing camps serve the many anglers who come in search of tyee, the 30 lb-plus chinook which are taken there in numbers every year. Though they fight deeper down than coho the size and power of such fish demand strong lines and big landing nets. Commercial trollers sometimes carry a .22 pistol to deal with the really big ones; on the inflexible wire lines used for commercial trolling such fish need only to shake their head to be free of the hook and the fisherman tries to draw them gently up before they do so and shoot them before attempting to set the gaff.

Although it is rarely rated with Atlantic salmon or steelhead as a freshwater gamefish chinook, like coho, can provide excellent sport in rivers. On big waters spring- or summer-run fish often move rapidly and can be caught well upstream in the main river or larger tributaries from early summer onwards. Smaller rivers which lack early runs can offer sport for a short spell in the late season.

In rivers chinook tend to lie in runs or pools of moderate to heavy flow from which they may be tempted with a variety of artificial baits. Big wobbling spoons, fished deep and slow, are favourites for fresh-run fish in the lower parts of rivers while in the higher reaches good sport can sometimes be had on small artificial flies in low-water conditions. On big waters such as the Columbia, large catches are often made from May onwards when the fish are normally present in good numbers both in the main river and some of the larger tributaries.

Mooching.

Herring strip and live herring rigs.

SOCKEYE SALMON
Oncorhynchus nerka

Names
The official name derives from an Indian word meaning 'best of fish'. Local names include redfish in Alaska and blueback on the Columbia. The freshwater form is known as the kokanee. 'Nerka', the scientific name, derives from the Siberian word for sockeye.

Distribution

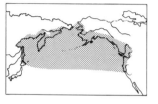

The sockeye enters streams and rivers from Hokkaido to the Anadyr river and from Alaska to central California. Its freshwater distribution is almost entirely limited to river systems which include lakes. Its centres of abundance are between the Bristol Bay area of Alaska and the Columbia River and on the Asian side around the Kamchatka peninsula.

The sockeye is the only Pacific salmon apart from the masu with a naturally occurring freshwater form, the kokanee. It is sometimes stocked outside its natural range for angling purposes or as a forage fish.

Size
Sockeye average about 6 lbs at maturity and have been recorded to 15½ lbs. The lake-dwelling kokanee rarely exceeds 1 lb; the angling record, from Echo Lake in British Columbia, weighed 9 lb 2oz.

Exploitation

The standard size, even shape and high oil content of the sockeye make it the ideal species for canning.

'God's gift to the canning industry', the sockeye was the first Pacific salmon to be commercially exploited on a large scale and it remains the single most important commercial species. The most productive North American river is the Fraser but those entering the Bristol Bay region of Alaska comprise the most important fishery, with annual catches commonly running between five and ten million fish. Principal methods of capture are by gill net, purse seine and trolling in the ocean approaches to spawning rivers.

Sockeye are only rarely caught by angling methods but the kokanee is an important sport fish in some lakes where it is taken on fly, bait or spinner.

Life Cycle
Sockeye fry emerge from river spawning gravels in spring and move quickly to adjoining nursery lakes. Most spend a year in lakes except in Alaskan latitudes where they may spend two or three years. Kokanee populations are usually but not always found in lakes with barriers preventing downstream migration.

In the ocean sockeye continue their lake feeding habits by a pelagic lifestyle in search of small crustaceans. They commonly range far into the Pacific and return after two years.

A phenomenon of sockeye runs is the occurrence of odd- and even- year cycles, differing significantly in numbers.

CHUM SALMON

Oncorhynchus keta

Name
Commonly called the dog salmon after its use by Alaskan Inuit as sledge dog food. The scientific name 'keta' derives from the vernacular in Kamchatka.

Distribution
The most widely distributed of the Pacific salmons except for the pink, the chum enters both streams and rivers from the Sacramento in California to the Mackenzie in Arctic Canada. In Asia, where it is most abundant, it occurs from Japan and Korea north to the Lena river in the Siberian Arctic. Chum have been introduced into the White Sea area of the USSR. There are no recorded landlocked populations and it has not apparently become naturalised in lakes.

Size
Chum average 8–15 lbs at maturity. The largest on record came from the Bella Coola river, British Columbia in 1951 and weighed 33 lbs.

Exploitation
The most important species in subsistence fishery, the low fat content of the chum makes it the preferred choice for smoke curing among Pacific coast Indians. It is also used as winter dog food in the north. As a commercial fish it is third in rank after sockeye and pink. Taken mostly by gill net, it is usually sold fresh or frozen; its low fat content makes it the least desirable species for canning.

As a sporting fish the chum is of least interest to anglers due to its plankton feeding habits at sea, its late return to the rivers and its lack of landlocked populations. It will sometimes accept small artificial lures in rivers.

Although not favoured for sea farming, the chum is the basis of a major ocean ranching industry in Japan.

Life Cycle
Chum fry migrate downstream soon after their springtime emergence from the gravel and by autumn most are leaving the coastlines for the open sea. They commonly remain in the ocean from three to five years, occasionally as long as seven, feeding largely on crustaceans, squid and small fish. They enter the parent waters in late autumn and on big rivers such as the Yukon may travel as far as 2,000 miles upstream. More typically they spawn in the lower reaches of rivers and in streams including very small creeks. Chum can also spawn successfully in the intertidal zone, as can pink salmon.

Fanged head of spawning male chum.

PINK SALMON
Oncorhynchus gorbuscha

Names
The official name derives from the distinctive pink flesh. It is commonly called humpback salmon after the striking shape of the spawning male. The scientific name comes from an Alaskan word.

Distribution

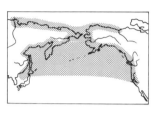

The most abundant Pacific salmon, the pink occurs from the Sacramento River in California to the Mackenzie in the Canadian Arctic. Like the chum it is most abundant in Asia and is found from Hokkaido and Korea north to the Lena river in the Siberian Arctic. It was introduced to the White Sea and has occasionally strayed into north-west European rivers. Though no naturally occurring land-locked populations are known the pink has a self-sustaining introduced population on the Great Lakes.

Size
Averaging 3–5 lbs at maturity the pink is the smallest Pacific salmon. The largest recorded weighed 14 lbs.

Exploitation
The pink is second to the sockeye in overall commercial importance and these two species are the staples of the canning industry. Most commercially caught pinks are taken by troll, purse seine or gill nets as they return to the coast. In subsistence fishing the pink is the least important salmon.

In sport fishing it is the third most important after the coho and the chinook. Although it comes a long way behind them in numbers taken, big catches are sometimes made at sea by coho fishermen from June onwards when they have reached adult size and are actively feeding on bait-sized fish. In river estuaries and along some beaches returning fish are sometimes taken on artificial flies.

Life Cycle
Pink salmon normally leave for the ocean immediately after their springtime emergence and, as with chum, the fry travel by night. After schooling in the estuaries they move into the open sea in autumn and often travel widely. In spite of their small adult size pinks will feed on fish as well as the invertebrates which support their early growth. They almost invariably return to the rivers after some 18 months at sea and their two-year total life cycle results, like

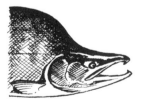

The main feature of the breeding dress of male pink salmon is the bizarre hump.

sockeye salmon, in two separate genetic populations. On most waters odd- and even-year cycles differ significantly in numbers.

Pinks usually spawn in the lower reaches of rivers and some do so successfully in the intertidal zone where the eggs are alternately washed by fresh and salt water.

MASU SALMON

Oncorhynchus masou

Names
Masu is the Japanese common name. An alternative English name is cherry salmon. The southern Japanese race, commonly known as the amago, is sometimes classified separately as *O. rhodurus*.

Distribution
The natural range of the masu is the Sea of Japan and adjoining areas. Anadromous masu enter streams from Pusan, Korea, north to the Amur river and the south coast of the Sea of Okhotsk; Japan except the south coast; Sakhalin, the Kuril Islands, and the southwest tip of Kamchatka. The ocean range is limited to the Sea of Japan and inshore waters adjoining Pacific spawning streams.

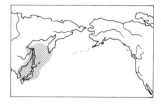

   The amago is widely distributed in fresh waters in the south of Japan. Non-migratory forms occur in some other parts of the masu range and a relict population exists in the mountains of Taiwan.

   The masu has been introduced to a few waters outside its natural range, mainly in the northwestern US.

Size
Anadromous masu return to the rivers at average weights varying from 2 to 10 lbs; individuals occasionally reach 20 lbs. Amago are relatively small but anadromous fish and those from some lakes may exceed 5 lbs.

Exploitation
Masu are of local importance both to commercial and sporting fisheries. The beautiful, red-spotted amago is a popular angling fish in Japan.

Life Cycle
Juvenile masu commonly spend a year in fresh water after their spring emergence from the spawning gravels. The smolts descend to the Sea of Japan and coastal waters of the Pacific Ocean and Sea of Okhotsk and reach 1 lb or more by the end of their first ocean year. In the following months they grow rapidly, often adding several pounds by the time they return to their home rivers. They normally return in the summer of their second ocean year but some either return after a few months or remain at sea into a third year.

A deep body shape is common to most masu as well as anadromous individuals of the closely related southern Japanese amago.

   Masu enter their parent streams from late summer and spawn relatively early, often from late July into August and September. The tendency for male salmonids to mature early is particularly marked among masu; a large proportion of males mature in the streams and never go to sea. Amago commonly migrate from spawning streams to feed in lakes or rivers; some populations enter the relatively warm waters off the south of Japan, feeding in brackish estuaries and bays to which they travel in autumn and return the following autumn or winter.

Haida village c.1900.

Status

In spite of their present abundance Pacific salmon are today usually estimated at only half the numbers of a century ago. Until then the native peoples of the Pacific basin had taken millions of salmon annually without apparently affecting the abundance of the fish. For the coastal Indians the Pacific salmon was as important as the buffalo was to the people of the plains; a single family was estimated to use a thousand sockeye salmon in a winter, while large quantities were traded with interior tribes along the old grease trails. Such numbers could only be taken by an efficient technology, and an indication of this was the fact that for the first century of European settlement the fishing remained in the hands of the Indians. The wide array of methods, including seines and gill nets, was such that in 1887 a US fisheries officer reported that 'the most modern appliances could not compete with the methods familiar to the natives'.

The state of the fishery changed quickly during the expansion of the canning industry in the early years of the twentieth century. Fishing pressure increased with the introduction of power vessels and larger nets. Settlers increasingly turned to fishing, adding to the Indian production or replacing it as people left remote villages for the new population centres. The effects of the commercial boom became obvious after the freebooting era of the Second World War, when the consequences of blatant over-fishing became apparent. For the first time it was generally realised that the supply of fish was not inexhaustible.

The salmon's freshwater habitat was also becoming threatened. The most famous single incident was the Hell's Gate disaster in the Fraser River Canyon in 1914. Rock slides caused by railway construction prevented that year's peak cycle sockeye run, estimated at over 37 million fish, from reaching the spawning grounds, an event from which the river had not fully recovered sixty years later. The Columbia's massive chinook runs were whittled away by the construction of dams and later expensive improvements including fish lifts were necessary to bring the numbers up to the half-million or so which now return annually to the system.

Damage to famous rivers was paralleled by the largely unseen degradation of small creeks used by coho and chum salmon. Thousands were swamped with timber debris or the spawning beds silted or washed out by the flash floods following logging operations. Pollution, the thoughtless erection of dams and barriers or the removal of gravel for construction wiped out whole runs or severely reduced the spawning potential of countless streams.

Conservation

Management of the Pacific salmon resource required not only local efforts but international agreements among the main fishing nations. The first step towards this was taken in 1937 with the formation of the International Pacific Salmon Commission. Established by the US and Canada to regulate the Fraser sockeye fishery from which both countries benefitted, a treaty agreement specified the equal division of research and river improvement costs and of the annual salmon harvest; its first project was the building of the Hell's Gate fishway in 1938. Pink salmon were later included in the agreement and the Commission soon led the way in the field of salmon research, including the highly accurate long-range forecasts of salmon numbers on which today's catch allowances are based.

On the opposite side of the Pacific there had also been changes. The Russian colonisation of eastern Siberia had led to an expansion of fishing activitiy there and after the Second World War Japan, long the leading Pacific fishing nation, began operating as far afield as the central Bering Sea. US and Canadian concern for their own stocks led in 1953 to the formation of NORPAC, the International North Pacific Fisheries Commission which made an agreement to abstain from taking stocks which were being maintained on a sustained yield basis by another country, as well as a fishing limit of 175° West for the Japanese ocean fleet. The need to ascertain the countries of origin of salmon visiting the central Pacific led to the largest ocean research project ever undertaken.

Today the Pacific salmon fishery is for the most part highly regulated. On the North American side high seas netting is banned and commercial fishermen are allowed to operate only in close co-operation with state and provincial research teams who decide on open times, catch limits and fishing locations for individual runs of salmon. A government buy-back scheme for fishing boats operates in some areas, with Indian fishermen being given preference in licence allocations; native fishermen still account for nearly half the commercial catch in addition to their own food fisheries. Angling restrictions now operate in some coastal areas as well as in fresh water. The management of the fishery has been further enhanced by major new research projects. In Japan, which has relatively few salmon rivers of its own, the ranching of chum salmon from hatcheries has led to the establishment of a new industry. British Columbia pioneered the successful use of artificial spawning channels and in 1976 initiated an ambitious Salmonid Enhancement Programme with the aim of re-establishing the salmon in their former numbers. Such developments have led to an increase in salmon in some areas and may eventually result in increased productivity in the Pacific fishery as a whole.

3 BROWN TROUT and SEA TROUT

Salmo trutta

Brown Trout

JUVENILE STAGES

1 The orange adipose fin and unspotted tail are characteristic. The parr marks are less clearly defined than those of the similar Atlantic salmon parr. Red spots are usually present, especially along the lateral line and, like the dark spots, are surrounded by pale halos.

RIVER ADULTS

2 Female Typical small head and smoothly rounded body shape. The anal fin of the female is slightly concave.

3 Male Typical sharp head, long upper jaw and slightly humped shoulder of mature adult. The anal fin is slightly convex, the lower jaw slightly hooked.

FORMS The appearance of brown trout may vary greatly even on the same water. Red spots are often absent and the dark ones differ in size and number. The tail is sometimes spotted, especially on the upper lobe. Local forms may have distinctive features.

4 Lake form With heavy marbling, common on many Irish loughs.

5 Rare Scottish form Gold and green colouring and fine speckles.

6 Silvery Norwegian form resembling sea trout.

7 On densely populated waters trout often retain parr marks through life. Small adults can be distinguished from juveniles by their relatively square-cut tails.

8 Fish from deep, weedless riverpools commonly have sparse spots. More rare are vermiculated markings on the back.

9 Ferox type Found mainly in big mountain lakes these are characterised by their large size and great age. Old males retain the hooked jaw year-round; females retain normal head proportions. A pelagic lifestyle is indicated by the slightly concave, sharply tipped tail. Big browns from rivers or lowland lakes are usually younger, with more thickset bodies and blunt, convex tails.

SCALE AND FINRAY COUNTS There are 14–19 scales (commonly 16) counted diagonally from adipose fin to lateral line. The anal fin has 10 or less separate rays.

FLIES From left: Greenwell's Glory, Coch-y-Bondhu, March Brown (hackled and winged wet flies); Blue Upright, Dark Olive, Royal Coachman, Brown Bi-Visible (hackled and winged dry flies); Pheasant Tail nymph.

PLATE V

Sea Trout

JUVENILE STAGES

1 Parr There is no distinction between brown trout and sea trout parr. On many streams small brown trout are in fact sea trout parr.

2 Smolt Found in streams only in spring and early summer, smolts can be recognized by their brilliant silver flanks, yellow pectoral fins and small size (usually under 8 inches (20 cm)).

3 Finnock Fish returning to fresh water in the same year as their first ocean migration can be identified by their small size (usually 9–12 inches (23–30 cm)) and delicate form. Entering streams from July onwards, most are sexually immature.

RETURNING ADULTS

Sea trout fresh from the ocean are bright silver with a prominent lateral line, white pectoral and anal fins.

4 Over-wintered Trout Sea trout entering streams in summer at around a pound in weight are generally maiden fish which have spent one winter at sea.

5 Large Fish These may be repeat spawners or maiden fish returning after two or more winters at sea. They are very variable in appearance but can be distinguished from Atlantic salmon by the long upper jaw, which reaches to or beyond the rear of the eye, and by the square-cut tail and the different scale count (see Brown Trout).

6 Coloured Fish Male showing typical sea trout coloration after 4–6 weeks in fresh water. Coloured sea trout can be distinguished from resident brown trout by their lack of clear, bright colours; they often turn a dull bronze-brown with faint halos around the spots. They have no true red spots but they develop rusty brown ones.

7 Breeding Male The hooked jaw varies in size with the age of the fish. The colour is variable; the back is usually green or brownish, the lower flanks dull yellow. Males are more strongly coloured than females and may be difficult to differentiate from male brown trout.

8 Kelt Well-mended kelts, found in rivers in spring, are often mistaken for fresh run fish; most can be identified by the thin shape and pale silver-white flanks.

FLIES From left: Teal Blue and Silver, Alexandra, Bloody Butcher, Grouse and Claret, Zulu (traditional wet flies); Sunk Lure (modern lures).

PLATE VI

1	2
3	
4	
5	
6	
7	
8	

Names

The common name derives from the colouring, compared with the silver of sea-run trout. In the US it is sometimes known as the German brown or Loch Leven trout after the places of origin of the first introductions. In Britain distinctive forms are sometimes named separately, e.g. Gillaroo, and large piscivorous browns are known as Ferox trout.

Sea trout is the common name for the sea-run brown; in Wales it is known as sewin and in Ireland as white trout. Small sea trout have local names, e.g. finnock, whitling or herling. The name slob trout, used for estuary-dwelling browns, derives from the Irish word for salt marshes.

Distribution

A native of Eurasia, the brown trout occurs naturally in streams, rivers and lakes from Iceland to Afghanistan. It is abundant in northern Europe and in many upland waters of southern Europe and the Near East. Its eastern limits are from the eastern slopes of the Urals south to the Pamirs. The most southerly natural population occurs in the Atlas mountains of North Africa. The brown trout is naturalised in much of North America and in parts of South America, Australasia, Africa and the Indian subcontinent.

Sea trout enter most streams and rivers in the British Isles and Scandinavia, parts of the European seaboard as far south as Portugal and tributaries of the Baltic, Black, Caspian and Aral Seas. Sea trout derived from introduced browns enter some rivers in North America, South America, Australia and New Zealand.

Size

Brown trout mature at sizes from a few inches upwards; on most waters wild rod-caught fish average 9–14 inches (23–36 cm). Rod-caught individuals over 30 lbs have been recorded from Europe, the USA, Argentina, Tasmania and New Zealand. In Europe commercially caught fish have been reported to 60 lbs.

Sea trout may return to fresh water at under 9 inches (23 cm) long; on most streams they average 1½–3 lbs but 10 lb fish are not exceptional. Sea trout over 20 lbs are rare but one of 46½ lbs was recorded from Suomenlahti, Finland in 1964 and individuals of the giant Caspian race have been known to reach 125 lbs.

Exploitation

In Europe the brown trout is the most important freshwater gamefish and worldwide it rivals the rainbow trout in popularity. The sea trout is the most respected game fish in Europe after the Atlantic salmon.

Brown trout are widely reared for planting in angling waters but rarely for eating due to their slow growth rate and poor domestic qualities compared to the rainbow trout.

Life Cycle

Brown trout fry emerge from the spawning gravels in spring and soon take up individual feeding territories. Although they enter fast currents to feed young browns prefer somewhat quieter water than rainbow trout and they tend to grow more slowly, commonly reaching 3–5 inches (8–13 cm) by the end of the first growing season. While many spend their whole lives in small headwater streams the majority of trout born in them will migrate downstream to better feeding areas in rivers or lakes. Where these fail to meet the territorial or growth needs of all the trout a proportion migrate where possible to the ocean, usually as silvery smolts of 5–9 inches (13–23 cm). The tendency to become smolts appears to be genetically determined with rivers having differing proportions of migrants.

Young brown trout have numerous red spots; on adults they may be sparse or absent.

Brown trout have been known to live for 23 years and quite often reach ages of five to eight years. The relatively long life expectancy means that they may grow slowly for the first few years but still reach a large size. Few are likely to exceed 3 or 4 lbs, however, on a purely insect diet. On rocky acid streams they rarely exceed 1 lb unless a regular supply of forage fish is present to maintain growth. Occasionally an individual trout will reach a large size by turning on its own kind but lakes which produce browns in excess of about 5 lb usually hold big shoals of oily forage fish such as the Arctic char which are a staple of ferox browns on the Scottish lochs. Sea trout normally grow fast on a diet of crustaceans, sandeels and other high-quality saltwater foods.

As the breeding time approaches mature males become darker in colour and develop a distinct hook on the lower jaw. Sea-run fish may enter spawning rivers from spring onwards but trout in lakes usually wait until early autumn before congregating at the mouths of feeder streams. In October and November most fish will be on the spawning beds located in rivers or streams, including very small headwaters, and occasionally along stony lake shores. Most brown and sea trout spawn annually with spent fish or kelts dropping slowly back to their feeding grounds over the following months. Although post-spawning mortality is a normal occurence many fish survive into the following year with repeat spawnings being common; sea trout have been known to spawn as many as thirteen times.

BROWN TROUT

Angling

The canny disposition of the brown trout has earned it the reputation of a 'fisherman's fish'. Most wary of the trouts, the challenge of its capture has made it a favourite among fly fishermen in particular. Its popularity through the centuries has also give the brown trout a special place in angling tradition and in the development of fishing tackle and techniques. Today its status has been greatly enhanced by widespread introductions which have resulted in naturalised populations providing prime fishing in many parts of the world.

SMALL-STREAM FISHING Browns are usually easier to catch on fast, rocky streams than anywhere else. These provide territories for large numbers of trout while intense competition for food means longer feeding spells and less cautious inspection of anglers' offerings. In rough water they also have less chance of being alarmed by the sight of the angler, while anything which looks edible must be quickly taken before being swept past by the current. Such waters are good places to get to know the basics of trout fishing as well as to make a catch.

On small streams a catch can be made on most days of the season providing the fish are not alarmed – even small browns on little-fished waters react very quickly to the sight of a moving angler. In clear water it pays to move cautiously upstream, casting ahead into likely places – pools, runs or pockets around stones. Small flies are deadly for this kind of fishing where banksides are open enough to allow casting; on overgrown streams the skilful use of a worm or other natural bait may be required. Spinning is of limited use in covering the small, shallow pools which typify rough stream habitat.

Small-stream browns commonly feed throughout the day but morning and evening often provide the best action in low water. Small floods or freshets with a little colour should be taken advantage of as these often fish best. In coloured flood waters browns can be as easy to catch as any other trout.

While fish on stony streams are generally numerous but small, those of slower lowland waters reach larger sizes. On chalk or limestone streams they commonly average 1 lb or more due to the relatively rich feeding found in such alkaline waters, as well as the smaller numbers of trout they may hold. In such streams brown trout have more choice of food and can be circumspect about taking a fly. They are more prone to selective feeding and a choice of wet flies, dry flies or nymphs, particularly in small sizes, may be critical to success.

RIVER FISHING Brown trout fishing on rivers offers more scope in angling methods than the small streams. Not only is there usually more space to cast a fly but more time can be spent on the larger pools or runs before the fish are disturbed. Likely areas can be

Small flies are standard for low water work. The traditional spider patterns of northern England, with their soft, sparse hackles, are deadly on stony streams.

Brown trout and dry fly: a classic combination.

covered from a distance and there is less emphasis on the careful stalking and close-range fishing demanded by the lesser waters. River trout, however, are often more particular in their feeding habits. In early spring they are slower to accept the anglers' lures than those of the lesser tributaries and through the rest of the season their feeding spells are punctuated by longer periods of inactivity. They can also be more selective in their feeding especially on the slower rivers, and success is more likely to depend on an understanding of their changing moods and behaviour. On fast, rocky rivers the best trout, but not always the best fishing, can be found in deep slow pools. In these they are particularly fussy and in low-water conditions may only feed well at dawn and dusk, or during good hatches of flies. On bright days better sport can usually be had by fishing the fast runs and pockets between pools where the trout can be as amenable as those on the small waters. In summer and autumn relatively large browns can sometimes be taken from shallow, broken runs or from behind stones.

On rain-fed rivers the best conditions for daytime fly fishing often occur during showery weather when the river carries enough extra water to maintain a supply of insects for the trout while remaining clear enough for the anglers' flies to be easily seen. When the water rises too much for effective fly fishing a spinner will often attract good fish, especially in the larger pools, while in heavy flood conditions natural baits such as worms or small fish can still account for heavy catches from sheltered eddies or against the riverbanks.

On spring-fed waters such as the famous chalk streams of southern England the lack of spates or freshets offers less variety in fishing conditions. Here the emphasis is on delicate presentation of small flies, often to an individual feeding fish. While fine leaders may be a necessity in tempting wild browns from clear, slow, spring-fed streams the prevalence of weed beds and the relatively large average size of trout require a balance in line strength.

LAKE FISHING Although stillwater habitats tend to be more uniform in character than rivers they vary from deep and relatively unproductive mountain lakes and impoundments to lowland waters with rich food supplies. It is in shallow water, which allows good sunlight penetration, that the bulk of the foods on which trout depend are produced and the best fishing is often found close to lake margins.

On many lakes boat fishing is the favoured way of covering the likely areas. The boat can either be positioned to drift across a given section of the lake with the wind, or rowed to cover spots where trout are seen feeding. In the absence of rising fish a wet fly can be employed to search such likely areas as the mouths of feeder streams, the margins of weed beds or, in open water, the wind lanes which commonly denote concentrations of spent insects. Bank fishing can be equally effective where good casting access can be found between trees or beds of aquatic vegetation. On stony, weed-free waters bank fly fishing is often effective on windward shores where the trout may feed on spent insects right up to the water's edge. In mixed fisheries containing both brown and rainbow trout they commonly feed deep and sinking lines may be needed to contact them.

The outsize, Ferox-type browns found in some deep lakes need special tactics. In early spring they can sometimes be taken on big flies or spinners from the shore but for the rest of the season they spend the daylight hours in the depths and trolling with big spoons or a natural forage fish bait is then the likeliest way of contacting them. In autumn they can also be taken as they ascend the spawning streams.

NIGHT FISHING Brown trout normally continue feeding after dark and night fishing can be particularly rewarding. Night fishing has a mystique of its own as bigger trout are often taken then than during the day.

Baits for night work should be bigger than those normally used in daytime. Very large dry flies work well, as do bulky wet flies retrieved very slowly but not too deep. Floating plugs, or natural baits such as worms or small fish drawn slowly across the surface, are often irresistible to brown trout at night. Whatever type of bait is being used a taking fish should be allowed several seconds before the hook is set.

Ferox brown trout and landlocked Arctic char, a useful forage fish.

The evolution of fly fishing

The practice of catching brown trout on artificial flies goes back to ancient times. In the third century the Roman writer Aelian described the taking of fish with 'spotted skins' in the mountain streams of Macedonia where 'fisherfolk wrap ruby-coloured wool about their hooks and wind about this two feathers which grow under a cock's wattles' – materials still in common use today.

In medieval Britain fly fishing was already an established practice. The first book dealing with the subject, *Treatyse of Fysshynge with an Angle*, was written by Dame Juliana Berners, a fifteenth-century prioress, and included detailed dressings for twelve trout fly patterns. Another important work was Isaac Walton's classic *The Compleat Angler*. First published in 1577, it remains the only fishing book widely known to the English-speaking public.

Trout fly pattern attributed to Dame Juliana Berners.

The practice of fly fishing, along with other forms of angling, expanded rapidly after the start of the Industrial Revolution. Its modern development began on the fast streams of Scotland and northern England with books such as William Stewart's *Practical Angler*, published in 1857, heralding a burgeoning new literature on the subject. The emphasis then shifted to the chalk streams of southern England where scientific developments in dry fly and nymph fishing were pioneered and the new fashion for tying imitations of particular insects was expounded in the erudite and prolific writings of Victorian authors like Frederic Halford and George Skues. Lord Grey's classic *Fly Fishing*, published in 1899, included fishing experiences both on the chalk streams and the salmon and sea trout waters of Scotland.

The related development of North American fly fishing is associated with the brook trout and the mountain streams of Pennsylvania and the Catskills. The first major American angling book, *The American Angler*, was published by Thaddeus Norris in 1864. Fly fishing for Atlantic salmon, rainbow trout and brown trout also featured in the development of the sport with men like Henry Van Dyke, Theodore Gordon and George La Branche adding to the quality of writing which characterises much of fly-fishing literature. The practice of fly fishing on the Pacific coast has been beautifully captured in the modern works of Roderick Haig-Brown.

While the basic method of fly fishing has changed little since the time of the ancient Greeks refinements in tackle and tactics, and the literature associated with it, have proliferated. The practice of fly fishing has spread worldwide and books on the subject appear in many languages. Many species of fish are now caught by fly fishers although the brown trout remains a favourite.

Status

The brown trout remains a common fish in most of its native range except in heavily industrialised regions where much of its habitat has been destroyed. In some northern mountain areas stocks have also been affected by increasing water acidification and important local races have also been lost by the indiscriminate planting of hatchery strains. Its tough, adaptable nature has, however, resulted in the establishment of many self-sustaining populations outside its native areas.

The brown trout is particularly abundant in northern Europe including areas north of the Arctic Circle. In the Lapland region of Scandinavia it occurs both in rivers and lakes with lake-run fish often reaching large weights; fish in the autumn run from Finland's Lake Inari commonly average 9 lbs and have been reported to over 33 lbs. Norway and Sweden both have trout fishing of similar quality and Iceland, at the western extreme of the trout's range, is known for its big river-dwelling browns.

Scotland has loch and river fishing in all areas with such famous waters as Loch Awe producing big Ferox browns. Ireland is world renowned for its quality fly fishing on Mask, Corrib and other loughs. Wales and England have extensive spate streams in addition to numerous put-and-take fisheries and the famous chalk streams of Southern England.

France has rough stream fishing in the hilly areas of Brittany, in the Pyrenees, the Massif Central and the fine chalk streams of Normandy. The Benelux countries have brown trout stocks in the Ardennes while in Germany good fishing can be found in several regions including the Bavarian Alps, the Harz mountains and the Eifel hills. Austria and Switzerland have good trout stocks in their Alpine waters with lake-run fish often reaching large sizes. Eastern Europe also has brown trout fishing, the mountain regions of Poland and Czechoslovakia being especially renowned. Spain, Italy and Greece all have trout in their mountain areas while Yugoslavia's Julian Alps are famous for quality fishing. Western Asia has some important but largely unexploited populations of brown trout in Turkey, Iran and north-eastern Afghanistan.

INTRODUCTIONS The most important plantings of brown trout outside Eurasia tooke place between 1864 and 1905. During this period trout eggs transported by sea provided the hatchery stock from which today's populations in North and South America, Australasia, Africa and the Indian subcontinent are descended.

Tasmania was first to receive brown trout. Conditions here proved ideal and today Tasmanian waters constitute one of the finest fisheries in the world. Another fishery was soon established in the Snowy Mountain region of the Australian mainland while New

Zealand's brown trout, also from the Tasmanian hatchery, established themselves on both islands. Although many New Zealand waters later proved better suited to rainbow trout the browns remained an important part of the famous sport fishery.

The brown trout of India and Pakistan are descended from Loch Leven stock first hatched in the Nilgiri hills in 1868. Today naturalised fish thrive in Kashmir and the snow-fed waters of Gilgit, Swat and Chitral in northern Pakistan. Loch Leven fry were introduced in the Drakensberg moutains of South Africa in 1890 and from there to Kenya, where year-round equatorial growth led to the establishment of an important fishery. The famous brown trout of Argentina and Chile derive from English and German fish arriving in 1904 and 1905 which quickly established themselves in Andean streams as far south as Tierra del Fuego.

THE BROWN TROUT IN NORTH AMERICA The brown trout is now a widely distributed and fully naturalised immigrant in 40 states in the USA and in parts of Canada. Deriving from eggs received from Germany in 1883 and Scotland in 1884, it quickly established itself in a number of eastern rivers. At first its presence was often resented due to its encroachments into the already dwindling brook trout habitats, but once its sporting potential was realised it gained quickly in popularity. Today it also plays an important part in public stocking policies; whereas planted rainbows are virtually all caught in the course of a season from heavily fished rivers most browns survive into subsequent seasons and offer the chance of catching big fish. Its old reputation as a cannibal is little justified; it is no more prone to eating other fish than other trouts but the fact that it is more difficult to catch, often survives to grow bigger, and lives longer means that it more often requires a fish diet to maintain itself.

While good brown trout fishing can be found in many parts of the US some of the most spectacular is in the western mountain regions where lake-run fish reach large sizes. Flaming Gorge reservoir in Wyoming has given up browns in excess of 30 lbs and large new impoundments in other areas hold populations of big and sometimes little exploited trout.

SEA TROUT

The appearance, habits and angling qualities of the sea trout are so different from those of the brown that it has acquired a status of its own. Its attracts a devoted following among European game fishers, with many preferring its sporting as well as culinary properties to those of the Atlantic salmon whose waters it shares. It has proved itself hardy and resilient and in spite of the heavy commercial fishing pressures which result in its wide availability in European stores as 'salmon trout' it continues to enter northern streams in big numbers. Populations derived from introduced brown trout have also established themselves in other parts of the world and the sea trout is now a recognised game fish in parts of eastern North America, South America and Australasia.

Sea trout tend to use small streams in which to spawn, either short coastal ones or the tributaries of rivers hundreds of miles inland. Each water has its characteristic sea trout migration pattern although it is only on the most barren coastal streams that all trout are likely to run to sea. On most waters a proportion, mainly males, remain as brown trout while among migrants the males tend to mature and return sooner than females; such facets of sea trout biology account for the fact that on many rivers most sea trout, and particularly the large ones, are females.

After a period of freshwater growth commonly lasting two or three years the young fish assume the silvery dress of the smolt. As with Atlantic salmon the smolt run takes place in spring while some streams also have a smaller autumn run of parr which do not turn silver until after they have reached salt water. Some of the spring smolts often return within a few weeks at 4–12 oz after feeding in nearby coastal waters; though most of these small sea trout are sexually immature many remain in the rivers for weeks or months before returning to sea.

Larger sea trout are either repeat spawners or mature maiden fish returning after one or more years away. Some will have spent their time in the ocean at no great distance from the home stream while others will have travelled hundreds of miles; the big sea trout of some eastern British rivers travel the North Sea as far as Norway. The biggest trout often return early in the year with a few rivers having small runs in April. The main runs usually occur in the months of May, June or July with smaller numbers entering in August, September and October. After autumn spawning the kelts drift back downstream to reach the sea during winter or early spring; their survival rates are normally high, and on many waters it is estimated that some 40 per cent will return to spawn the following year.

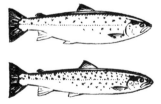

Adult sea trout returning to fresh water vary in the amount of spotting and in shape; maiden fish are often deeply built, previous spawners may be long and lean.

Angling

The sea trout is renowned not only for its beauty and size but for its spectacular performance on the line. Wild and shy on its return to the river, it can be a free taker to standard angling methods during periods of high water while at night, when it can be caught even in drought conditions, its sporting qualities are often represented by fly fishermen as being 'what fishing is all about'.

STREAM AND RIVER FISHING The big summer runs are the basis of sea trout fishing from May or June to the end of the season. The earlier runs which enter some rivers in April are rarely sought after due to the small numbers of fish, although some are caught by salmon anglers. The large size of these early runners, often from 5 lbs to as much as 20 lbs, sometimes leads to their being mistaken for spring salmon.

The start of the main runs generally coincides with the high tides of May in southern areas or June further north. Rain also encourages the fish to enter fresh water but, unlike salmon, they do not rely on it and sea trout will move upstream by night even while rivers remain low. On most waters the first arrivals consist of large fish often averaging 3–5 lbs, with a sprinkling of others in the 1–3 lb range. July may see a predominance of these lesser fish while in late July or early August the smallest, half-pounder class of sea trout enter many streams and continue running into the autumn. Larger fish may accompany them while on some rivers the late season sees a further run of big ones.

After their entry into fresh water sea trout tend to be unsettled and move around a good deal. A stretch which holds big shoals one day may be devoid of fish the next; some may return again to the estuary while others run upstream to settle for periods up to several weeks in holding pools. They often shelter in deeper and slower water than salmon and are attracted by bankside lairs overhung by trees. While water levels remain low it is from such places that they can be tempted, sometimes by the use of small flies or baits fished on fine tackle during the daytime but much more predictably at dusk and through the night.

Night fishing has a charm of tis own but to be appreciated it requires a different approach to daytime angling. Ideally a shoal of sea trout should be located during the day and the fishing area checked for snags which will be invisible during darkness. The shoal should not be disturbed before nightfall, although a fish or two may sometimes be taken at dusk from the neck of a pool without disturbing the area below.

At darkness the sea trout leave their safe lairs and rove up into the heads of pools and down into the tails, where they often lie in shallow water and can be tempted by a fly fished across the stream.

Night fishing for sea trout, a popular activity on British rivers.

Night lures for sea trout from top: Medicine Fly, Secret Weapon, surface lure.

They usually show themselves at night by periodic rises but rather than chasing after them it can prove more effective to work slowly, waiting for the fish to pass within casting range while avoiding the hasty movements which can turn a potentially successful night's fishing into a series of tangles and bankside hook-ups. The use of a light is best kept to a minimum since it interferes with night vision; many anglers do without one since even on the darkest nights enough light remains for fishing while delicate operations such as tying on flies can, with practice, be done entirely by touch. By remaining in one familiar stretch of river tackle problems can be minimised and, provided the trout are not unduly disturbed before dark, one or two pools usually suffice for a night's fishing.

Sea trout are easiest to tempt when they are newly arrived in the river or have just settled into a new pool. At these times they are usually taken on standard sea trout flies, including those specifically designed for night fishing, but the longer they remain in one place the harder they can be to tempt and small flies, including brown trout patterns, become increasingly effective. Although the use of artificial flies is by far the most popular method for night fishing natural baits can also be used. An unweighted worm drawn slowly across the surface, or just beneath it, can be deadly; when a fish takes it should if possible be allowed to move off without hindrance for several seconds before the hook is set. During daytime sea trout are notoriously moody. A good rise in the river level, however, encourages them to become active and less choosy about the anglers' offerings; fish which are resting while moving upstream in high, coloured water can give excellent sport.

While the river remains suitable for fly fishing most sea trout patterns are likely to score. Small bar spoons are also effective at this time, and many anglers find that upstream spinning can be more effective than the conventional down-and-across technique. In flood water a bunch of worms, which sea trout are known to be particularly fond of, is usually reckoned the most effective natural bait.

STILLWATER FISHING Lakes are attractive holding areas for sea trout and on river systems which include them they tend to remain within their bounds until the approach of spawning time. Some of the most productive sea trout fisheries are based on big stillwaters with such famous places as Scotland's Loch Lomond and Loch Maree giving up thousands of good fish annually. As in rivers sea trout are easiest to tempt when fresh from the sea but local knowledge can be important to fishing big waters since the fish normally frequent particular areas and avoid others. On such waters most fishing is done from boats and common methods include dapping, in which a big fly is skipped on the surface, as well as standard wet fly techniques.

SEA AND ESTUARY FISHING In some regions sea trout feed along shorelines in sufficient concentrations to make rod fishing for them worthwhile. Notable locations include Scottish and Norwegian sea lochs and fjords, Danish coastlines and parts of the Finnish archipelago. Bright streamer flies, spinners and natural sandeel baits are commonly used in saltwater fishing.

Estuary fishing is also locally important. Flies, spinners and natural baits will take sea trout on estuaries; the best locations are usually pools at the upper tidal limits. Estuary fishing is especially attractive when low water makes daytime fishing in rivers a poor prospect; tidal movements have the effect of regular spates and while sea trout may not take well while the tide is up the periods immediately prior to its arrival and immediately after its departure are often productive.

Even when they have been in fresh water for several weeks sea trout retain angling qualities distinct from those of resident browns. They take a fly or bait violently and react instantly to the touch of the hook, often leaving the water in a series of high, vertical leaps and making fast, erratic runs. Good reflexes are needed in handling them, especially when they are just in from the sea; then they have soft mouths from which the hook tends to pull free.

When they are in a good taking mood sea trout are not shy of heavy nylon or large baits. At other times they can be difficult to tempt even on the finest gear and are renowned for following the bait without taking it cleanly, a habit which has led to the creation of a number of successful fly patterns which include small hooks projecting behind. In low water sea trout can best be tempted during daylight hours by very small flies or by natural baits on fine tackle fished close to a stationary shoal.

In Europe Atlantic salmon are quite often encountered while fishing for sea trout, and a choice often has to be made whether to fish heavier gear in case one is hooked or to concentrate on success with the sea trout. Where salmon do not run particularly large a line or leader of about 8 lb breaking strain will suffice for both species during high-water conditions.

In low water sea trout shoals can often be spotted from above.

Status

The sea trout has generally suffered less from man's interference than the Atlantic salmon. Less valuable as a food fish, its commercial exploitation is on a smaller scale while its coastal migrations allow it to avoid ocean netting. The sea trout also makes use of smaller streams for spawning and it will enter both streams and rivers during low water, allowing good escapements while salmon remain vulnerable to inshore nets as they patrol river mouth areas waiting for rain.

Like most salmonids the sea trout has lost some important waters due to pollution or damming while the increasing acidification of spawning streams has put some populations at risk in the northern strongholds of Britain, Ireland and Scandinavia.

BRITAIN AND IRELAND The sea trout is once again abundant in most British rivers following the UDN disease which hit sea trout and salmon stocks in the late 1960s and 1970s. The Irish Sea populations are especially renowned with Welsh rivers enjoying a particular reputation. The top 20 Welsh rivers provide some 20,000 fish to the rod each year including many in double-figures. The Dovey and the Conwy are noted producers of fish up to 20 lb. In Wales the large fish enter most waters in May with smaller school sea trout running through June and July. The most important sea trout regions of England are in the south-west and the far north. The rain-fed rivers of Devon and Cornwall have runs starting in May while on northern streams the main runs begin in June. The north-west has many spate waters including such productive rivers as the Lune and the Border Esk while the north-east has several good rivers including the Wear and the Coquet which, in addition to summer runs, also have autumn ones including the outsize fish once known as bull trout.

Though better known for its salmon, Scotland has quality sea trout fishing throughout the country including the productive Solway rivers, numerous west coast and Hebridean streams, the saltwater voes of Orkney and Shetland, and big east coast rivers. Scottish sea trout average around 2 lbs with some waters noted for much larger fish; the Tweed has an unusual run of very big sea trout with a salmon-like life cycle.

A number of Irish rivers have good sea trout runs. One notable exception is the Shannon, the largest river in the British Isles which, like other rich lowland waters, attracts trout to remain as freshwater residents. East coast streams produce sea trout with growth rates similar to the Welsh rivers which share the Irish Sea feeding grounds. The Atlantic coastline has numerous sea trout waters including the well-known Burrishoole system in County Mayo, and many loughs.

NORWAY Most Norwegian rivers have good runs and in those rivers which lost salmon stocks following the introduction of the parasite *Gyrodactylus salaris*, sea trout have become more important. Most feed, and are sometimes caught, in the extensive fjords which comprise much of the country's coastline. The main catch is taken in rivers from mid-July, when the main runs begin, through September. On small Norwegian waters sea trout average 1–3 lbs but on big rivers like the Laerdal they may average 10 lb with occasional specimens over 20 lbs.

ICELAND Iceland has runs of sea trout on most rivers but the best known are those of the south and west. The most prominent are probably the Ranga and Skafta systems, the Öfusa-Hvita estuary and the Straumfjiardara and Stadara rivers of the Snaefellsness area. The latter rivers have early runs of very large sea trout but the main runs throughout Iceland are in July and August. The Stadara is primarily a sea trout water but on most other streams sea trout may be taken along with Atlantic salmon or sea-run Arctic char. Icelandic sea trout have been known to exceed 20 lbs; average sizes vary from 1 to 5 lbs.

SWEDEN Baltic sea trout are renowned for their large size and Sweden's most important salmon and sea trout water, the Morrum river, has produced rod-caught fish to 33 lbs. The average size here is commonly over 8 lbs and on the Dalaven river, another important water, about 4 lbs.

FINLAND Finland's only notable Baltic sea trout river is the Tornio but they are sometimes taken from brackish water locations in the extensive Åland archipelago. Sea trout are also found in some north-flowing streams in Finnish Lapland.

Denmark is known for its large sea trout taken from saltwater locations around the coast. Germany and Holland have only a handful of small sea trout streams but Brittany has a number of rivers with quite good runs, as do Spain and Portugal. Most of the important Spanish salmon rivers of the Asturia region have good sea trout runs.

Naturalised sea trout occur in several parts of the world. A rod fishery exists in parts of New England and the Maritime Provinces of Canada; derived from introduced browns, these North American sea trout commonly run to a good average size and have been known to reach 28 lbs. They are reported occasionally from the Pacific coast.

In South America there are several long-established populations in southern Patagonia and the Falklands. Like other naturalised populations they do not appear to move far from river estuaries but nevertheless reach large sizes; in the Falklands fish of 15–20 lbs are common. Tasmania and New Zealand both have good, though little publicized, sea trout runs.

4 RAINBOW TROUT and STEELHEAD

Salmo gairdneri

Rainbow trout

1 Parr Characteristic small oval and rounded parr marks. The body, dorsal fin and tail have numerous small dark spots; there are no red spots. Young rainbows can be separated from the similar cutthroat trout by the lack of teeth at the base of the tongue.

ADULTS Mature rainbow trout can usually be distinguished from other salmonids by the pink, red or lilac stripe along the flanks. The tail is fully spotted and the upper jaw extends only to the rear of the eye or, in some males, slightly beyond. Some coastal rainbow trout populations have small red or orange cutthroat marks beneath the lower jaw.

2 Adult male Outside the breeding season the sexes can be difficult to differentiate but the male has a slightly sharper head and longer upper jaw.

3 Adult female Typical small, rounded head.

4 Breeding male Large, old fish in spawning colours. The pink lateral stripe often extends as a deep red or purple flush across the flanks; the colour is particularly strong on the gill covers. On young males the enlarged snout is less prominent.

FORMS Some races of rainbow trout have distinctive appearances due to local environmental conditions or to genetic differences.

5 Kamloops rainbow trout. The main lake-dwelling form in the interior lakes of southern British Columbia is distinguished by bright, silvery flanks, blueish back and small ,sparse X-shaped spots. When planted outside their native range older fish may lose some of the characteristic features.

STOCKED RAINBOW TROUT

6 Hatchery fish Typical fin mutilations. The stunted tail and bent leading edge of the dorsal fin are characteristic; the pectoral fin is often completely missing. Heavy artificial feeding often gives a deep, slab-sided appearance but loss of body condition may follow stocking. Grown-on trout regain more natural fin shapes but can usually be distinguished by twisted leading rays of dorsal fin and outside rays of tail.

PLATE VII

1
2
3
4
5
6

FINRAY AND SCALE COUNTS There are 120–180 scales along the lateral line. The anal fin has 10 or less separate rays.

FLIES From left: Adams, Grizzly Wulff, Nations Special, Spratley Fly (wet flies); McGinty, Ginger Quill (dry flies); Muddler Minnow and Mickey Finn (hairwing flies).

Steelhead

JUVENILES

1 Parr These are no different from resident rainbow trout parr. On coastal streams small rainbows are often the parr of steelhead.

2 Smolt Silver colouration prior to migration.

3 Half-pounder Individuals returning to streams after their first few months at sea are recognized by their small size, usually 10–12 inches (25–30 cm), deeply forked tails and delicate form. Most are sexually immature.

RETURNING ADULTS Fresh-run steelhead have bright silver flanks, steel blue backs and whitish lower fins. There is a strong demarcation line between the dark upper body and the silver flanks. There are small, distinct black spots on body, dorsal fin and tail; on the back and flanks these are very variable in number. The pink rainbow stripe is usually absent.

4 Summer steelhead Typical appearance at return from the ocean. The sexes are often difficult to differentiate by external features. They are very variable in size; some waters have runs of small, one-sea-winter steelhead of 1–3 lbs in weight.

5 Winter steelhead Male fish showing early development of the pink rainbow stripe after entry into fresh water. The male head changes – elongated snout and small hook on lower jaw – are becoming apparent. Winter fish are less variable in size than summer steelhead; they are normally 5 lbs or more in weight. They may enter rivers from autumn through to May.

6 Male in breeding dress The red flush on the flanks often extends down to the belly; the gill covers are bright red. The jaw enlargement is variable – big, old fish have distinct hooks on the lower jaw.

7 Kelt or spent fish Appearance soon after spawning. The thin body, distended vent and dark colours are characteristic. Kelts are found in rivers in spring and early summer.

Note: Adult steelhead can be told part from Pacific salmons by their troutlike features including nearly square tails, thick tail stalks and short anal fins; from sea-run char by their dark spots and shorter jaws (the upper jaw extends to, or just beyond, the rear of the eye).

FLIES From left: Skykomish Sunrise, Boss, Polar Shrimp, Spruce, Kalama Special, Comet, Royal Coachman Buck (wet flies); Steelhead Bee (dry fly).

PLATE VIII

1	2
3	
4	
5	
6	
7	

Names

The common name derives from the 'rainbow' colours. Distinctive freshwater forms often have local names, e.g. Kamloops trout. The Latin name is derived from Dr Meredith Gairdner of the Hudson's Bay Company. The Latin name *Salmo mykiss* is applied to the main Asiatic form.

Steelhead is the common name for sea-run rainbow trout.

Distribution

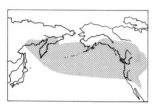

A native of the Pacific basin, the wild rainbow trout occurs widely both as a freshwater resident and as the migratory steelhead. It is found from the mountains of north-west Mexico to the Bering Strait and southwards on the Asian shore to the mouth of the Amur. In North America it does not occur naturally east of the continental divide. Introduced to temperate freshwaters worldwide, naturalised populations now exist in North America east of the continential divide, in South America, Australasia, Africa, the Indian subcontinent and Europe.

Size

Mature rainbow trout vary from a few ounces on small streams to 10 lbs or over on big lakes and rivers. Wild fish on most angling waters average 9–14 inches (23–36 cm). The largest on record appears to be a Kamloops strain fish which had been introduced into a small virgin water, Jewel Lake in British Columbia. One of two outsize rainbows caught during an angling competition, it weighed over 52 lbs.

Steelhead rainbows vary on their return from the sea from a few ounces to 20 lbs or more but on most rivers average 3–9 lbs. The largest on record was angled in 1970 by an eight-year-old boy fishing from a dinghy in the ocean off Ketchikan, Alaska and weighed 42 lbs 2 oz.

Exploitation

The rainbow trout is the most widespread game fish of western North America and it rivals the brown trout as the most popular worldwide. Its freshwater form is the staple quarry for trout anglers while the sea-run steelhead is the most prized trophy of Pacific rivers.

Neither type is much exploited commercially although in some areas the steelhead is taken as a by-catch in salmon nets or local food fisheries.

As a farmed fish the rainbow is by far the most important of the trouts. It has long been the standard species for the food market and is the main trout used in stocking put-and-take fisheries.

Life Cycle

The eggs of the wild rainbow trout are normally laid in spring in contrast to the autumn spawning habit of most salmonids. The warming of the streams at this season encourages development of the eggs, and hatching occurs within a few weeks. The young tend to grow quite rapidly and on natural streams often reach 4–6 inches (10–15 cm) by their first winter. They have a higher metabolic rate than brown trout and a higher oxygen requirement; they commonly grow about 15 per cent faster. Rainbows are fond of fast water, frequenting stronger currents than those preferred by other trout or char and thereby reducing competition when these species are present.

Young rainbow trout: the rounded parr marks are typical of species which live in fast water.

The rainbow trout is known for its wandering habits. Even in rocky coastal streams, however, where most are genetically programmed to migrate to sea, a proportion usually elect to remain in the same way as brown trout in equivalent waters. Some spend their lives in headwater streams while others move down to better feeding areas in rivers or lakes before returning to spawn. Although some have been known to live up to seven years, the life expectancy of the rainbow seldom exceeds five and good feeding is necessary from an early stage if fish are to attain a large size. They tend to feed heavily on small invertebrates even as adults but few reach weights in excess of about 3 lbs without the easy availability of large and nutritious prey creatures. The exceptional growth of rainbows in some lakes in the Pacific Northwest relies on plentiful shoals of small kokanee salmon while naturalised populations in many South American rivers reach large sizes by feeding on abundant freshwater crabs as well as forage fish.

As spawning time approaches mature rainbows become dark, their flanks turning purple or mauve and the male often developing a kype. Most spawn in small streams but rivers are sometimes used and, in rare cases, the wave-washed shores of lakes. Though rainbows are spring spawners the exact timing varies with local climatic conditions. The elevation of a stream has a direct influence and in California it has been reckoned that, thanks to the extremes of climate between coast and mountain interior, rainbows may be found spawning somewhere in the state in every month of the year.

Annual spawning is common among those resident in fresh water. Steelhead rainbows have been known to spawn up to four times but rarely spawn more than once; post-spawning mortality among these migrants is usually high and although survival rates of around 30 per cent have been recorded five or ten per cent is more typical, particularly on rivers where steelhead return at a large size.

RAINBOW TROUT

Floods offer trout a varied menu by washing out creatures from bankside and stream bed.

Angling

A free taker to fly, spinner and natural bait, it is for its dramatic performance on the end of a line that the rainbow trout is renowned. No other salmonid fish can match the initial spell of high-speed leaps, cartwheels and tailwalks which epitomise the fight of the wild rainbow trout. Its angling qualities together with its wide availability for stocking purposes have ensured a worldwide popularity. While put-and-take rainbow fisheries serve the needs of millions of urban anglers, the native fish of the Pacific slope and naturalised populations elsewhere provide the most desirable fishing in terms of quality.

The rainbow is generally regarded as being easier to tempt than its popular rival the brown trout. It is certainly easier to approach and when alarmed will recover faster. It is also less cautious when it comes to bait size and presentation. The wild fish, however, is by no means an easy quarry. It has the same feeding cycles as other trout and the better class of fish is often hard to hook. In some waters it can also be distinctly selective in its choice of fly.

SMALL-STREAM FISHING Wild rainbow trout on stony headwater streams are characterised by their large numbers and small individual size. Like other trout in such places they are relatively easy to catch, and the emphasis on this kind of water is on attractive surroundings and pan-size fish. As in all clear-water trout fishing a cautious approach is necessary, preferably from downstream, but trout here will seldom be selective in the matter of lure and bait.

Where gradients ease and the stream settles into a gentler rhythm with good pools larger fish can usually be found. On well-populated acid streams the average size is still likely to be under 10 inches (25 cm) but on the alkaline creeks and springheads rich food supplies often mean much larger trout.

Small-stream rainbows often feed freely during daytime fly hatches but dawn and dusk are the likeliest times to find the larger fish active, particularly in low-water conditions. A rise in the water level tends to bring trout of all sizes on the feed and on rain-fed streams a summer spate or freshet carrying a little colour is the most auspicious time for a big catch.

A short rod can be an advantage in the brush and timber confines which characterise many such waters. A longer rod, however, gives better line control, especially in fast water, and on more open streams a length of 8–10 ft (2½–3 metres) may be more appropriate.

RIVER FISHING White-water fly fishing is the classic technique for rainbows in big, fast rivers. Large bucktail or hairwing flies, originally developed for use in the mountain rivers of western North America, are used in the fast currents often favoured by feeding rainbow trout. In many such waters they reach several pounds in

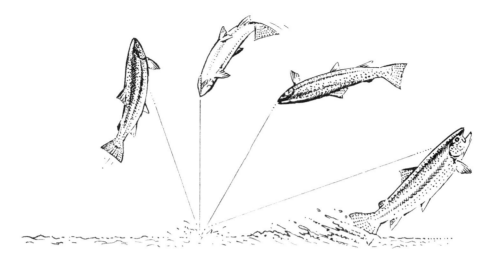

weight and a big fish coming to a fly at the surface, followed by an acrobatic fight in heavy water, is one of the most sought-after experiences in trout fishing. The big flies developed for this western style of fishing are the basis for many popular patterns now used for stillwater rainbows and for salmon, char and other trouts in a variety of different environments.

Typical aerial fight of wild rainbow trout includes high-speed cartwheels, left, and tailwalking.

Smaller flies of more traditional pattern are more commonly used for rainbows in the slower reaches of rivers and in lakes. Hook sizes 10 or 8 are standard on most waters, somewhat larger than those commonly employed for brown trout. Although few traditional rainbow trout patterns are intended as accurate imitations of particular insects there are times when good representations can pay; on fly-rich waters such as the famous limestone streams of Pennsylvania rainbows are often selective in their choice of food, and even on fast western American rivers characteristic insect hatches such as the big local stoneflies can produce better fishing to imitative patterns.

Traditional rainbow trout flies are more bulky than those used for brown trout.

Spinning is also a popular method for wild rainbows and for general fishing a broad range of spinners, spoons and small plugs can be used. Feeding fish often take these artificials well while on hot summer days, when they may not be active, a bright spinner will sometimes provoke them into striking when fly or bait fail to attract.

Natural baits are particularly useful on overgrown streams where dense cover precludes the use of other methods. Bait fishing is widely practised on open waters as well, and a standard North American technique is bottom fishing with salmon egg bait. While this static method sometimes accounts for good catches it is rarely as attractive to the sight-hunting trout as a moving bait, particularly in moderate currents where a variety of natural insects, worms, small baitfish or, where allowed, salmon eggs, can be drifted along the river bed with deadly effect.

LAKE FISHING The feeding cycles of rainbows in lakes are often more obvious than in running water, with heavy rises being followed by hours of inaction. When the fish fail to show at the surface roving tactics can be used to search out different water depths and small nymphs fished from the bank on fine, long leaders may tempt trout either from marginal shallows or deeper water. On many lakes the use of a boat can be an advantage, particularly in areas like the Pacific Northwest where heavily timbered shorelines and extensive weedy shallows often make bank fishing impractical.

A common way of searching out feeding rainbows on western lakes is by trolling an artificial fly from a small boat or canoe. A wet fly is drifted ten or twenty yards behind the craft as the angler paddles slowly along shorelines, weed beds, across the mouths of feeder streams or along wind lanes. Where trout are found to be feeding the fly can be cast over them in the normal way. Spinners or plugs can be fished in a similar fashion while bait, usually worms, is often used in combination with a small gang troll, the flashing action of which can attract fish from a distance. During winter ice fishing with bait or small jigs is a popular sport on many lakes.

Fly fishing can be practised on high-level waters or those in far northern areas throughout the season. Those at lower elevations, however, often heat up during summer to the point where trout, in daytime at least, must be searched out by deep trolling in the cooler depths. Though less interesting, this method can have its rewards in the size of fish. Big, deep lakes such as those in the famous Kamloops country of western Canada commonly hold rainbows well into double-figure weights. Like big brown trout these rely on forage fish for their growth and either natural baitfish or an imitation can be trolled at various depths until fish are contacted.

Stillwater rainbows are often caught as they congregate at the mouths of spawning streams. The spring runs on large tributaries can be highly productive and on waters like the Great Lakes, where the fish can average several pounds, angling pressures are often intense. Probably the most famous fishing of this kind takes place at the mouth of the Tongariro, the main feeder to New Zealand's Lake Taupo, where thousands of outsize rainbows are taken annually.

PUT-AND-TAKE FISHING The fast growth and easy rearing of the rainbow trout make it the ideal species for put-and-take angling. Fisheries authorities as well as commercial fish farms often rear trout for this purpose and artificial trout fisheries are a common feature of the angling scene. Farmed rainbows usually differ from wild ones in that selective breeding from mixtures of native strains have resulted

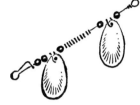

Gang troll

The small kokanee, or landlocked sockeye salmon, has been widely planted in western US lakes as a forage fish for trout.

in semi-domesticated fish which lack some of the desirable character and appearance of the natural forms. Their feeding behaviour has also been influenced by the artificial feeding routine of the fish farm while fin mutilations testify to the densely crowded conditions in which they are raised. The main angling attributes of stockie rainbows are their ease of capture and the large size at which they are sometimes introduced.

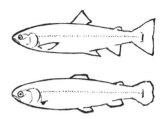

Wild rainbow trout (top) and freshly stocked hatchery fish showing typical fin shapes.

The majority of waters receiving regular introductions of farmed rainbows are in lowland areas with relatively good natural food supplies. If stocking levels are kept in balance with the removal of trout by anglers the fish are able to maintain good condition, and on lakes and impoundments which are stocked for long-term benefit rather then straight put-and-take fishing they can be introduced in numbers low enough to allow good seasonal weight gains. Many such waters hold other species of fish whose fry provide a major food source in addition to whatever invertebrate life is present, although the potential size of trout still depends on management decisions regarding the number of fish to be stocked.

Rainbows which survive the first few months in their new surroundings regain some of their wild qualities. Though they still lack some of the finer points which make for top quality fishing, grown-on rainbows adopt natural feeding patterns which make their capture more challenging. Their fighting qualities often improve and their fins, though rarely regaining their pristine condition, repair themselves to a large degree.

The ultimate angling lure for freshly stocked rainbows is an artificial fly tied to represent a feed pellet. Such fish, however, have little fear of humans and will often remain in shoals while freely accepting almost any kind of bait or lure which anglers standing only yards away care to offer them. Once the fish have developed natural feeding, however, more skill is required to take them. Attractor flies or seasonal fry imitations are popular stillwater lures while standard fly, spin or bait fishing methods are all likely to account for grown-on trout.

Status

The wide availability of farmed rainbow trout has meant that in terms of numbers the species not only remains common in its native areas but has been successfully established in many other parts of the world. In terms of quality, however, the wild rainbow trout has suffered, particularly in the southern part of its range where habitat degradation, over-fishing, and the introduction of genetically different stock fish have resulted in the extinction or impoverishment of important native races.

The southernmost populations of wild rainbow trout in North America are found in the mountains of north-west Mexico. In California it is found in streams of the Sierra Nevada in the southern half of the state and in almost all lakes and rivers in the northern half, including such famous fisheries as the Pit, Feather, Kern and McCloud Rivers. Most waters are periodically planted with stock fish and while California is not noted for producing outsize rainbows, they have been reported to at least 18 lbs. Further north, the huge Columbia river system dominates river fishing in Oregon, Washington and Idaho with big tributaries such as the Deschutes and the Snake being renowned for their excellent fishing. Lake Pend Orielle, in Idaho, produced the world fly-caught record of 37 lbs. Alaska has outstanding fishing for wild rainbows in a few areas, notably the lower reaches of rivers entering Bristol Bay where the eggs and fry of the region's abundant sockeye salmon promote fast growth.

Western Canada is unique in the extent of its native rainbows. The southern interior of British Colombia is the home of the Kamloops race, famed for its fighting qualities. It can be caught in most of the region's numerous lakes, while further north the less well-known caribou country has fishing of similar quality. Wild rainbows are found in virtually all the rivers of the province with several, including the Babine and the Thompson, being noted for large fish. Alberta has native stocks of rainbows in the Athabaska system and naturalised or planted fish in many other areas.

INTRODUCTIONS The rainbow trout began the first of many long journeys beyond its native range in 1874 when Seth Green and Fred Mather, the first culturists of the species, succeeded in transporting fertilised Californian eggs by sea around Cape Horn to New York. Rainbows were soon planted in many rivers in New York, New Jersey and Pennsylvania; before the end of the century fish from New York hatcheries reached Michigan and then the Rocky Mountain states, which at that time were still devoid of the species. Although planted fish would remain a standard feature, self-sustaining populations of rainbow trout soon succeeded in establishing themselves, often at the expense of native brook trout, in several eastern areas.

Over the next 50 years rainbow trout reached every continent. In South America, Shasta strain trout from California provided the original brood stock for the famous fisheries in Chile and Argentina. Introduced in the first years of the twentieth century, rainbow and brown trout both reached enormous sizes in the absence of local predators or rival species. Although average sizes are now less than they were the huge South American fishery still rivals any in the world. Chile has hundreds of quality rivers and streams in the 1,000 miles (1,600 km) of mountainous coastline south of Santiago. Those close to towns have the greatest angling pressure and, while many produce trout up to 20 lbs, the best fishing is commonly found in the wilder regions of the country. In Argentina, which has a similar extent of waters, the main angling centre is Bariloche. Thousands of big rainbows are taken annually from the huge Lake Nahuel Haupi near the town while there are numerous other waters both to the north and the south. Other important rainbow fisheries exist in Peru, notably Lake Titicaca, and in some Colombian lakes; in Ecuador a number of high-altitude lakes have self-sustaining populations of rainbow-cutthroat hybrids.

New Zealand has a reputation for naturalised rainbows rivalling that of South America. Here too they are descended from Californian stock which arrived at Lake Taupo in 1883. As in South America sizes nowadays are less than they once were but an average of 3 lbs is common and twenty-pounders are still taken regularly from some lakes. The Taupo system in the North Island provides the most outstanding fishing but big rainbows are found in most areas of the country. Another important southern hemisphere sport fishery is centred in the Snowy Mountain region of south-eastern Australia.

The equatorial highlands of Kenya and Tanzania have a long established fishery which produces rainbows of a high average size. The Himalayan region of Kashmir has some rainbow trout but the best fishing is found in the rivers and lakes of Gilgit and Swat, in the North-West Frontier Province of Pakistan, where naturalised rainbows reach large sizes.

Europe has an abundance of rainbow trout waters though most rely on hatchery fish to maintain stocks. Probably the best known are English lakes and reservoirs such as Grafham and Rutland Water which produce big numbers annually; grown-on fish in excess of 5 lbs are not uncommon in these rich lowland waters. Scotland has some unusual rainbow fisheries based on fish farm escapees which have been known to exceed 20 lbs.

STEELHEAD

The steelhead has acquired a reputation which rivals that of the Atlantic salmon. The most prestigious gamefish of Pacific rivers, it attracts a dedicated following wherever it is found. Though probably no easier to catch than Atlantic salmon – few anglers average one fish per visit on most waters – the size, beauty and fighting qualities of this capricious sea-run rainbow trout are sufficient to maintain the enthusiasm of its numerous devotees.

Classic steelhead rivers are fast and rocky, with good spawning tributaries and deep holding pools to shelter the adult fish on their return from the ocean. Such waters are rich in territories for small fish but poor in food supplies for adults, a characteristic which discourages growing fish from staying within their bounds; the sea-going habit of steelheads is not as fixed as that of salmon and the presence of lakes or extensive food-rich areas on a river system will tempt a proportion to remain as freshwater rainbows. It is only on relatively short and shallow coastal streams that virtually all the fish will run to sea, usually after one or two years of freshwater growth. The steelhead's variable migration pattern extends to its ocean life as well. Like the European sea trout some return after only weeks or months to give the half-pounder runs characteristic of some streams. Others spend between one and three years on their ocean travels, gaining weight rapidly in offshore surface waters; some steelhead stocks feed as far afield as the central Pacific before returning to the rivers of their birth. Like other trout, and unlike salmon, they continue to feed in fresh water.

On most rivers the main runs take place in winter and early spring, shortly before the spawning period, while the less common summer-run fish may spend up to a year in fresh water before spawning. Some rivers have small atypical runs entering at unusual times, a phenomenon which points to the ability of the species to adapt itself to the great environmental changes which have been taking place in the Pacific basin over the ages. Although the timing of the steelhead's return to the river is believed to be determined largely by inherited instincts, local climatic conditions play an obvious part with a rise in the water level encouraging the fish to enter fresh water.

Relatively little research has been done into the life history of the steelhead thanks to its minor importance in the commercial fishery. Its considerable sporting value, however, has led to an increasing interest in its conservation and enhancement. Wild steelhead stocks have dwindled dramatically in the past 50 years and the loss of many summer runs in particular has been a matter of growing concern.

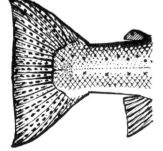

The crescent shape of adult steelhead tail reflects long ocean travels. The steelhead's tail wrist is broader than that of any other salmon.

Angling

The majority of steelhead are taken as they ascend the rivers to their spawning grounds in winter and early spring. Their resting places during this migration are often deep in swift currents, and while they can sometimes be taken on fly the heavy water conditions common in these seasons usually demand the use of weighted baits. The principal baits for winter steelhead include a wide assortment of artificial and natural offerings, fished on gear strong enough to suit the size and strength of the fish as well as the nature of its rivers.

Basic winter steelheading gear consists of a long and powerful rod in combination with a strong reel loaded with 10–20 lbs test monofilament. Fixed-spool, baitcasting or multiplier reels are often used although on rough rivers many steelheaders prefer quality centrepins such as the Hardy Silex which, while requiring skill in casting off the drum, offers better fast-water line control than geared reels.

Among many specialised artificials designed for steelhead the only common denominator tends to be the use of red and orange. While these colours are known to attract most members of the salmon family their use for steelhead has become almost mandatory; fish are sometimes caught on a hook simply adorned with a red rag. Many artificials also imitate salmon eggs, to which steelhead are known to be partial. Often used in combination with tufts of coloured wool these represent either single eggs or clusters. On many western rivers the most popular are the 'spin-n-glo' types which include spinning vanes. These attract not only by colour but by their rapid vibrations and are particularly effective in murky flood water when the bait cannot easily be seen. Other popular artificials include plastic worm imitations and a range of spinners, spoons and

Steelhead retain the acrobatic qualities of rainbow trout but are usually much larger. On most waters they average 5 to 10lbs.

Artificials for steelhead include egg imitations, spoons and plastic dew worms.

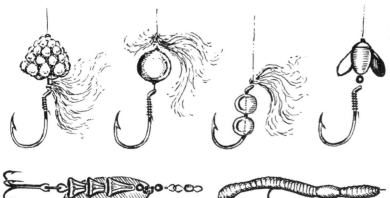

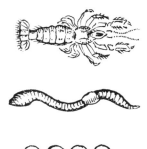

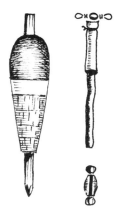

Popular natural baits –
ghost shrimp, worm and
salmon eggs.

Pencil lead, clincher lead
and steelhead bobber.

plugs. Favoured natural baits include prawn and ghost shrimp, worms and, where permitted, salmon eggs.

Both natural and artificial baits are fished beneath a float or bobber, or else by drift fishing in which the terminal gear bounces freely down the river bed. Weights used for the former method are normally simple shot or clincher leads while for drift fishing a pencil lead, attached to a weak line or inserted into rubber tubing, allows for minimum snagging on stony ground.

Since steelhead rarely show themselves at the surface the angler usually has to rely on careful coverage of likely holding areas. In big pools they commonly gather in loose shoals, spreading out to take advantage of places where depth and current speed suit them. Like Atlantic salmon they do not favour still water and are typically found in deep areas adjoining fast currents or beneath the currents themselves; typical spots are around the necks or down the main bodies of pools and in deep runs against rock faces. Since current speed at the river bed is slower than at the surface they can be found lying in what appears from above to be impossibly fast water. Large pools may hold numbers of fish but individuals can often be found sheltering in potholes behind stones between the main holding pools.

The take of a steelhead may vary from a gentle pluck to a savage strike but the setting of the hook is immediately followed by a line-stripping run. Unlike the Atlantic salmon, which often uses its great power in a drawn-out, subsurface struggle, the steelhead typically engages in a fast, acrobatic fight and frequently leaves the water in a series of twisting leaps. Instant reflexes are a decided advantage in dealing with these manoeuvres but however competent the angler a large proportion of fish will be lost to failed hook-holds. If the tackle holds, however, a steelhead will exhaust itself in a fairly short time. A beaten fish may be beached, lifted by the gills or netted; tailing is not recommended since steelhead, like all trout, have thick tail wrists with poor gripping qualities.

The best fishing conditions occur during periods of high water, the prime time being as the river clears following a flood. At this stage running fish will have begun to settle down in the holding pools and for a day or two may take the angler's offerings freely. During spells of settled weather with low water they become increasingly dour and success at these times will depend increasingly on a cautious approach and skilful use of relatively light tackle.

SUMMER STEELHEAD Summer conditions offer the angler a broader choice of methods than the cold waters of the early season and as rivers warm up the fish rise more freely to offerings presented above the river bed. It is the summer steelhead which is of particular interest to the fly fisherman.

Traditional steelhead flies are mostly hairwing patterns containing the bright shades of red or orange favoured for other artificials. Smaller sizes fished on floating lines are commonly used for low-water work while larger sizes, used in combination with sinking lines, are usual in high water. Most fly-caught steelhead are taken by standard wet fly methods, but summer fish will sometimes rise well to dry flies and new patterns are being increasingly used for this desirable way of taking them.

Summer steelhead runs are highly valued resources and the better-known US and Canadian streams are often regulated by fly-only restrictions or by catch-and-release policies. Some of the larger and better-regulated waters give excellent returns and big catches can sometimes be made; in Washington and Oregon, where hatchery-reared steelhead provide much of the sport, the emphasis is often on large numbers of fish averaging 5 or 6 lbs. Most waters from northern California to Alaska produce big fish as well, the best known of them in western Canada where wild fish commonly average around 10 lbs. The largest recorded fly-caught steelhead was taken in 1967 from British Columbia's Kispiox river and weighed 33 lbs.

Steelhead and dry fly.

Rivers with canyon sections provide observation points for locating steelhead during low water conditions.

Status

Although steelhead enter most north Pacific rivers many populations have been decimated since the early years of the twentieth century. The main reasons for this are usually seen as commercial over-fishing combined with habitat degradation, notably the destruction of spawning streams by logging operations and building of dams.

Summer steelhead runs have suffered particularly badly, and while man's interference can be seen as the cause of a general steelhead decline the demise of summer stocks, like that of the spring run Atlantic salmon, may be due to other factors as well. The migration patterns of anadromous trout and salmon are known to be affected by climatic factors and changes in ocean temperature are believed to result in natural changes independent of man.

In the US wild steelhead are occasionally found as far south as the Ventura river, which was once a good steelhead water, but more commonly from San Luis Obispo County, in central California, northwards. Large numbers enter the Sacramento system, the main river providing good fishing in late autumn and the tributaries through the winter. The most important coastal streams in California are the Russian, the Eel, the Mad and the Klamath which provide sport in autumn and winter. The Eel is also known for summer steelhead and the Smith for big fish to 20 lbs or more.

In Oregon and Washington fishing centres on the Columbia system which is regarded as the centre of steelhead abundance. The huge runs which enter it are now due to some extent to the large-scale plantings of hatchery-reared fish which have enhanced steelhead stocks in these states in recent years. Although the average size of these fish can be relatively small larger ones are not uncommon on some tributaries as well as on coastal rivers such as Oregon's Rogue and Umpqua. In Washington the sporting catch averages over 150,000 fish a year with nearly half comprising summer-run steelhead. Most are taken from the Columbia system including tributaries such as the Snake, and from such famous coastal streams as the Skykomish and the Stillaguamish.

British Columbia is best known for its very large wild steelhead from rivers such as the Skeena, the Kispiox and the Sustut. These northern waters resemble top Norwegian salmon rivers in character and their steelhead parallel salmon in their long ocean migrations. Most streams in the province have good runs with winter fish commonly averaging 9 or 10 lbs. In some northern rivers summer-run steelhead also average large sizes while on smaller coastal streams they may vary from 2 to 10 lbs or more.

In Alaska the steelhead is less common although good fishing is possible in streams in the south of the state and occasionally in the Bristol Bay region.

Conservation

It has long been recognised that the sporting value of the steelhead in most parts of North America far exceeds its commercial potential as a food fish and it is now largely conserved for angling. In some areas commercial fisheries still affect stocks by incidental captures in nets set for salmon but today many steelhead populations are more likely to be affected by anglers than by netsmen.

Enhancement efforts are concentrated on artificial propagation, regulation of angling and habitat improvement. Propagation has proved successful on major steelhead rivers in Washington and Oregon in terms of numbers although the short sea life of most hatchery fish has often led to a decrease in average sizes. Steelhead stocks in other areas rely to varying degrees on planted fish although wilderness rivers such as those of northern British Columbia and Alaska are rarely stocked. These are for the most part lightly fished and although they are naturally less productive in terms of numbers than those further south a large average size of fish is sufficient to maintain their reputation for quality.

Angling regulations for steelhead have become increasingly stringent in recent years both in the US and Canada and reflect an increased awareness of conservation needs, not only on river systems as a whole but on their individual parts. Waters with marginal stocks may be subject to complete closure or to short opening times. Daily as well as seasonal catch limits apply in most areas and punch cards or fish tags, issued with licences, are used to record all fish caught. Many waters also have fly-only or other restrictions on fishing methods.

River improvement is the most important long-term enhancement measure for steelhead as for other salmonids. It is also the most difficult to implement since most freshwater systems are under regular threat from a variety of human activities within their watersheds, and the widespread damage which has already been done can be extremely costly to rectify. Some limited success has been achieved by the creation of artificial spawning channels but the future status of many wild steelhead stocks relies on an increased public awareness of their environmental needs and a willingness to improve riverine habitats.

5 CUTTHROAT TROUT *Salmo clarki* and RARE TROUT

Cutthroat trout

JUVENILES

1 Parr Fish over 4 inches (10 cm) usually have the characteristic red or orange streaks below the lower jaw; parr marks are variable in shape. Fingerlings may lack the red outthroat marks but have tall, slim parr marks which distinguish them from young rainbow trout.

SEA-RUN ADULTS

2 Male in ocean dress The silver sides are typical; the red cutthroat marks may fade or disappear in salt water but the lower flanks and fins usually retain a golden yellow cast. The small spots on flanks, tail and fins distinguish cutthroat from Pacific salmon or sea-run dolly varden char.

3 Female in river dress The silver ocean dress is rapidly replaced by fresh-water colours including red cutthroat marks and green-and-gold flanks. Coastal cutthroats resident in fresh water have more compact spots.

4 Male in breeding dress A dull reddish or purple flush develops on the flanks and gill cover and a small hook usually appears on the lower jaw.

FRESH WATER FORMS Local races and sub-species of interior cutthroats have distinctive appearances. They are usually less densely spotted than the coastal type and their spots are often concentrated towards the tail.

5 Yellowstone cutthroat Sparsely spotted and with a reddish tinge on gill covers and flanks.

6 Paiute cutthroat A native of California's Silver King Creek, the Paiute is small and brightly coloured with few if any spots on the body.

7 Rio Grande cutthroat Once widespread in the Rio Grande system this colourful race is now isolated in remote headwater streams.

8 Lahontan cutthroat Native to the primordial Lahontan Lake area of the Great Basin this race reaches large sizes. Lake-run specimens may be silvery on the flanks.

Note: Cutthroats often hybridise with introduced rainbow and golden trout. Pure bred fish can usually be distinguished from rainbows by their colouration, longer upper jaws, and the presence of hyoid teeth at the base of the tongue.

FINRAY AND SCALE COUNTS There are 115–180 scales along the lateral line and 8 to 11 separate rays in the dorsal fin.

FLIES For sea-run cutthroats, from left: Mysid, Spider, Minnow Fly, Peter Ross, Green Ghost, American Coachman, Yellow Belle, Teal and Red.

PLATE IX

1	
2	
3	
4	
5	
6	7
8	

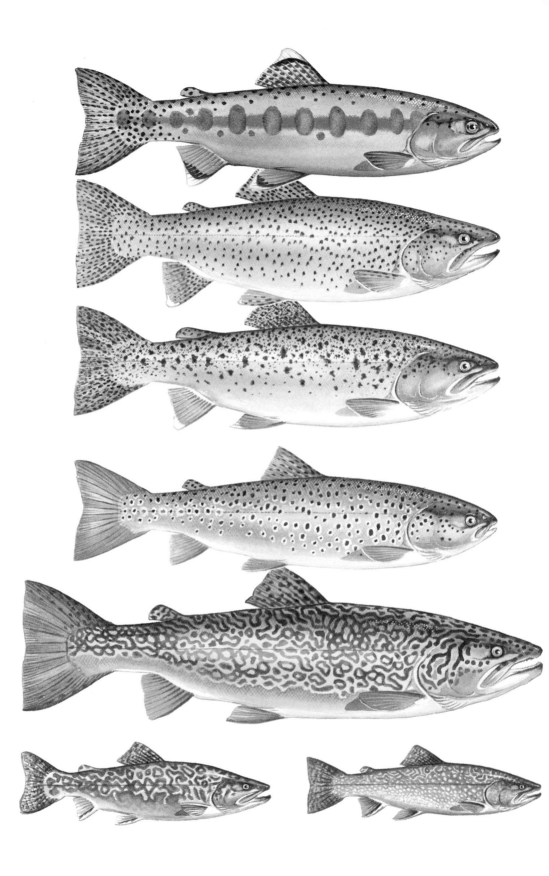

Rare Trout

NORTH AMERICAN SPECIES

1 Golden Trout Several forms of golden trout are found in mountain streams in the western US and northern Mexico. Wild California goldens are small and brilliantly coloured with red gill covers and lower fins, yellow and red flanks, and strong parr marks. Dorsal, pectoral and anal fins have contrasting black-and-white edges. Spotting on the body is variable but usually sparse. Native to the upper Kern River, the Californian golden is now found in several western states; in some waters golden/cutthroat hybrids are common. In hatcheries goldens lose the bright markings but retain a yellow cast to the body.

2 Apache Trout A deep-bodied fish, the Apache is distinguished from the similar Gila trout by the regular spots on body, dorsal fin and tail. A native of Arizona's White Mountains it now occurs as a planted fish in other areas.

3 Gila Trout The distinguishing marks of the Gila are its profusion or irregularly sized spots on body, dorsal fin and tail, and its very long adipose fin. The body is yellowish, sometimes with a rosy lateral stripe. A yellow cutthroat mark is sometimes found beneath the lower jaw and the dorsal, anal and pelvic fins are tipped with white. It lacks hyoid teeth at the base of the tongue. Once common in the Gila and Verde rivers of New Mexico, the Gila is a protected species in its remaining native creeks.

EURASIAN SPECIES The best known of several distinctive relict species are found in rivers and lakes on the Mediterranean watersheds of Italy, Greece, Yugoslavia, Turkey and Lebanon.

4 Softmouth Trout The unique underslung mouth distinguishes this Yugoslavian species. It occurs mainly in the Neretva river and its tributaries.

5 Marbled Trout Pure-bred fish can be recognised by the distinctive markings. It is found in several large Yugoslavian rivers, notably the Moraca where it has been recorded to at least 46½ lbs in weight. Hybrids between marbled and brown trout are now common in some waters.

HYBRID TROUT AND CHAR

6 Splake A cross between two chars – the brook trout and lake trout – the splake occurs mainly as a hatchery introduction in northeastern American lakes.

7 Tiger Trout This is a hybrid between brown and brook trout. Hard-fighting and easily caught, it is sometimes produced in hatcheries for stocking put-and-take fisheries.
Note: Both these hybrids can occur in the wild.

PLATE X

1	
2	
3	
4	
5	
7	6

CUTTHROAT TROUT

Names

The common name derives from the characteristic orange or red linings of the paired grooves beneath the lower jaw. Important inland races are usually prefixed by local names, e.g. Yellowstone cutthroat. The Latin name derives from Captain William Clark of the Lewis and Clark expedition. Sea-run cutthroats are sometimes known as harvest trout.

Distribution

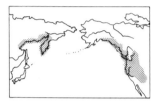

The cutthroat shares a similar Pacific range to the rainbow trout. Unlike the rainbow, however, it occurs naturally on the eastern slope of the North American continental divide including the upper drainages of the Missouri and Rio Grande systems. Today the Yellowstone region is the main inland stronghold of the cutthroat.

The coastal form is more widely distributed both as a freshwater resident and as a sea-run fish. It is common in many coastal streams and the lower reaches of rivers from the Eel river in northern California up to southern Alaska. It is also known on the Asian side of the Pacific basin.

The cutthroat has rarely been introduced outside its native range and only a few small naturalised populations exist elsewhere.

Size

Cutthroats mature at various sizes according to environment. In small streams they may never exceed a few ounces but in rivers and lakes they sometimes reach weights in excess of 10 lbs. The Lahontan race once produced the largest average size of trout in North America; the biggest authenticated cutthroat, a Lahontan angled by John Skimmerhorn from Pyramid Lake, Utah, in 1925, weighed 41 lbs.

Sea-run cutthroats taken on rod and line are usually between 8oz and 3 lbs in weight. Two-pounders are common but fish over 4 lbs are rare; the largest on record weighed 17 lbs.

Exploitation

Large commercial fisheries once existed on big lakes in the western US but today the cutthroat is valued purely as a sporting species. The inland forms are important in western wilderness areas while the sea-run cutthroat is a popular gamefish on Pacific coastal streams.

Fish culturists have found the cutthroat trout difficult to rear, and its tendency to interbreed with hatchery rainbow makes it of little use for stocking waters where hatchery rainbows are already present. Native cutthroat strains however, are propagated in some areas to enhance natural stocks.

Life Cycle

Like the related rainbow trout the cutthroat is a spring spawner, its fry emerging from the gravel within a few weeks and taking up individual stations behind small stones. Young cutthroats show a preference for slow-moving water, a characteristic which persists through life. This results in a partial division of the stream between the cutthroat and its common rival, the fast-water-loving rainbow trout, a similar division to that between brown trout and Atlantic salmon. The cutthroat is on the whole less strongly migratory than the rainbow and while both species tend to move downstream towards better feeding grounds, a larger proportion of cutthroats are likely to remain in headwater streams.

The growth rate of the cutthroat is generally slower than that of the rainbow but its life expectancy slightly longer. It is usually regarded as having a stronger tendency towards piscivorous feeding, and while the diet of stream-dwelling fish consists largely of invertebrates big lake-dwelling as well as sea-run trout include a large proportion of fish in their dict. The food of sea-run cutthroats consists mainly of small inshore species and the young of offshore fishes as well as juvenile Pacific salmon. The latter are of particular importance and the size of sea-run cutthroat populations in coastal streams can be directly related to that of their salmon. The trout take stray salmon eggs in fresh water during autumn and winter and migrating smolts in the estuaries during spring and summer, and streams which lose their salmon runs commonly show a severe decline in their cutthroat population.

The red cutthroat marks are used in threat displays towards rivals.

The migratory instinct of the sea-run cutthroat, like that of freshwater residents, appears to be less strongly developed than either rainbow or brown trout. While steelhead rainbows move out into the ocean, often for considerable distances, the cutthroat travels along the shorelines and although individuals have been known to travel 100 miles (160 km) or more most are believed to spend their sea lives in and around the estuaries of their parent streams.

Sea-run cutthroats usually spawn in small coastal streams and the lower tributaries of rivers. Inland forms also favour small streams but some spawn in larger rivers, such as the Yellowstone, and rarely along the wave-washed shores of the lakes. February – April is the usual breeding period and annual spawning is the pattern for most populations.

Angling

The shy nature, distinctive colouring and relative rarity of the cutthroat have an exotic appeal which makes for a different fishing experience than that associated with its extrovert relative the rainbow trout. A popular gamefish in some western areas, inland races of cutthroat are now the subject of conservation measures designed to enhance their numbers.

SMALL-STREAM FISHING Much of the best inland cutthroat fishing available today is in mountain headwater streams and high lakes where native fish still thrive in environments untainted by pollution or the introduction of farmed rainbows. Prime waters are often remote from roads but once reached can be rewarding both in terms of catches and in the beauty of their location.

Wilderness cutthroats are usually free takers, responding readily to a well-presented fly or bait. They favour somewhat slower waters than rainbows and on fast streams are commonly found in the tails of pools or in areas adjoining swift currents. Numerous but mostly small in size they can be taken on lightweight outfits which make for maximum sporting pleasure as well as easy carrying in rough terrain.

A special attraction in fishing remote mountain watersheds is that many hold unique strains of cutthroat, often brilliantly coloured fish rivalling the golden trout in appearance.

Telescopic rod – ideal for mountain hiking.

RIVER FISHING Tempting cutthroats from big, fly-rich rivers can be more challenging than on small waters. On the famous catch-and-release rivers of the Yellowstone region they can be selective feeders and small flies tied to represent seasonal insects may be needed to take them. Where angling pressures are less intense they tend to be less choosy, and like brook trout they can be particularly attracted to big, bright hairwing flies as well as spinners, plugs or natural bait.

In rivers where they are the dominant species big cutthroats can be found feeding in heavy currents as well as the quieter water with which they are usually associated. Their performance on the end of the line, though often powerful, is typically less acrobatic than that of the rainbow.

LAKE FISHING Still water cutthroats commonly reach a good size both in some high alpine waters and in big western lakes. On small lakes wet flies, dry flies or nymphs can take fish well but on larger waters big streamer flies imitating the forage species on which they feed can be more effective.

Status

While the coastal cutthroat remains abundant in most of its native range many interior forms have been decimated. The species has proved especially vulnerable not only to the standard catalogue of habitat degradations – chemical and thermal pollution, water abstraction, damming and over-fishing – but also to the introduction of other species, especially planted rainbow trout. While cutthroats do not normally interbreed with wild rainbows they commonly do so with genetically mixed farmed strains and the distinctive character of many local races has been weakened or lost in the resulting hybridisations. This problem is now more widely appreciated and some pure cutthroat strains have come under the protection of the law.

In the states of Utah, Montana and Wyoming the cutthroat remains relatively abundant. The Yellowstone Park fishery is renowned for the size and number of its fish and also for the success of its catch-and-release regualtions. The upper Snake river system is also known for it quality fishing, both in the main river and such famous tributaries as Henry's Fork and Jackson's Hole, while in neighbouring mountain areas of Montana and Wyoming many smaller waters hold healthy populations of cutthroat.

The Lahontan basin of northern California and Nevada still has mixed populations of the huge Lahontan race: the lakes in this area are believed to be the remnants of an extensive Pleistocene sea, the several unique cutthroat forms found around this basin deriving from ancient sea-run forms. The most famous of these, the Pyramid Lake cutthroat, may no longer exist as a pure race since the degradation of its spawning river. In 1938, the last year in which it was able to spawn, the 200 specimens collected averaged over 20 lbs. The big Lake Tahoe form is also believed to be extinct due to the building of irrigation dams on the Truckee River and the introduction of lake and rainbow trout.

Efforts have been made to repair damage done to Pyramid Lake using near-pure Lahontan fish and in recent years this water has once again been producing big cutthroats in excess of 10 lbs, while one original Lahontan-related form, the beautifully coloured little Paiute trout, still exists as a transplanted fish in a few streams. Mixed Lahontan strains still provide good fishing in California's Lake Independence and a few other big lakes.

Most other western states also have unique cutthroats, the remnants of once-abundant forms which owe their distinctive character to long isolation in remote headwater streams. Populations still thrive in high lakes and headwaters of major rivers including the Columbia, the Missouri, the Rio Grande and the Colorado.

Paiute cutthroat.

SEA-RUN CUTTHROAT

The sea-run cutthroat has a mystique of its own. The classic trout of Pacific estuaries and shorelines, its wide distribution and sporting qualities offer much potential for the angler. Though often overshadowed by the big steelhead and salmon which share its streams it has a dedicated local following with fly fishermen in particular finding its almost year-round availability a special attraction.

Habits

Sea-run cutthroats typically spend two or three years as stream-dwelling juveniles before migrating into salt water. By late spring they will be in the estuaries feeding mainly on aquatic invertebrates and terrestrial insects. At this time their characteristic green and gold body colours become increasingly obscured by a silvery layer of guanine, and after a few weeks the appearance of small cutthroats may be confused with the young of other Pacific species – salmon, steelhead or Dolly Varden char.

The stickleback, a staple for cutthroats in estuaries and inlets.

The larger fish also move into the estuaries after the spring spawning period, their migrations often taking place at the same time as that of the salmon fry and smolts which form an important part of their early season diet. While big cutthroats may continue to enter estuaries with the tides throughout the summer they often move off to adjoining beaches, bays or inlets in search of sticklebacks or other forage species. Commonly upwards of 12 inches (30 cm) in length, these larger trout can often be seen at the surface as they hunt the shorelines in shoals of ten or twenty.

By late summer mature cutthroats begin congregating again around the river mouths. The largest fish are often the first to enter fresh water, their migration typically coinciding with that of the returning coho salmon, but the main runs take place in September when the 'harvest trout' move into the streams in big numbers and a wide range of individual sizes from under half a pound to 3 lbs or more. As with other sea-run trouts, however, the composition of runs and their precise timing may vary considerably between individual streams. Most mature cutthroats spawn in early spring but some over-winter in the sea and numbers can sometimes be found in the estuaries throughout the winter season.

Sea-run cutthroats give sport on the fly both in fresh and salt water.

Angling

Sea-run cutthroat fishing is concentrated in and around the lower reaches of rivers and streams. Success depends very much on locating shoals moving in and out with the tide, along neighbouring shorelines or, in the late season, in upstream freshwater pools. Once found they can usually be tempted by an appropriate presentation of fly, spinner or bait.

Fish moving into an estuary with the tide can sometimes be spotted by their feeding movements at the surface. Initially they may move up at the head of the tide but their movements vary considerably and there are likely to be times, especially during the summer months, when the larger fish fail to appear. The unpredictability of estuary fishing has its rewards, however, in its challenging nature and in the various other species of fish which may be encountered. In addition to the cutthroats which are the staple quarry of estuary anglers, big streamer flies or small spoons may at different seasons also attract coho and pink salmon, steelhead or Dolly Varden char.

Streamer flies are standard for salt water work, small wet flies for river pools.

The roving tactics which commonly prove successful for estuary fishing can be extended to adjoining coastlines. The trout often patrol these for several miles while remaining close enough to the shoreline to be cast over, and in prime feeding areas, where the cutthroat shoals pass back and forth at frequent intervals, sport can be had throughout the summer months.

Many estuaries and beaches can be fished efficiently from the water's edge but there are some places where a boat can be a necessity including inaccessible rocky or timbered shores as well as areas in the US where legal access can be barred below the high-water mark. Boat angling extends the scope of fishing methods; fly or spinner can be used in the usual way while light trolling with these bait or with a worm fished behind a small gang troll, can be useful in seeking out the shoals.

For most cutthroat anglers peak fishing comes in autumn as the trout are moving back into the streams. Although they may be present in numbers their location is still an important factor since the shoals regularly shift pools. Sea-run cutthroats tend to lie in slow, deep water and by searching such likely spots as sheltered undercuts, around pilings and in the tailwaters of pools the angler will be covering likely ground. Heavy tackle is unnecessary for this type of fishing since sea-runs, although they fight well and frequently leap when hooked, rarely exceed 4 lbs

Although sea-run cutthroat are found in northern California and southern Alaska their main north American range is Oregon, Washington and British Columbia.

RARE TROUT

In addition to the rainbow, brown and cutthroat there are a number of rare trout species with localised distributions. Most are distinctively coloured fish living on the periphery of the trout's natural range, often in a single stream or watershed. The rarity and exotic appearance of such fish as the golden and marbled trout has attracted the attention of anglers while their genetic peculiarities and unique distribution have made them the subject of study by biologists.

The precise origins of these rare trout is often a matter for speculation. Most are clearly related to one or other of the three major species but it is not always clear whether they have evolved from them directly or whether some are more closely related to older forms. Recently developed techniques of genetic examination, however, have shed new light on their relationship with the common species while their geographic locations have given indications of their origins; in both North America and Eurasia they are found only along the margins of Pleistocene glaciation.

The principal freshwater range of today's major species comprises northern areas which were covered by ice up to 10,000 years ago. In the relatively short time since their recolonisation of these areas they have developed numerous local races, yet of the ancestral forms which preceded them no obvious trace remains. These were doubtless decimated during the glaciation periods but living species derived from these ancient forms may exist among some of the rare trouts which have survived in isolated mountains south of the main glaciation areas. This isolation could have enabled them to survive not only geographic and climatic changes but also hybridisation with the modern forms which have had regular opportunities to interbreed during the periods of sea migrations when they recolonised northern freshwaters.

Although a few trouts are believed to be relics of pre-Pleistocene forms most, like local races of char, are likely to have evolved from their commoner relatives through gradual adaptation to isolated habitats. Many are small, with strong colours and a tendency to retain territorial parr markings through life, a reflection of their crowded confinement in small streams.

Many local races have become extinct in recent years through the agency of man. The conservation of rare salmonids is a matter of urgency and as yet only a few areas have taken their protection seriously. Apart from their interest to anglers and naturalists, these fish are commonly the result of adaptation to extreme climatic conditions – high temperatures, acidity or alkalintiy or water – and could prove useful in fish farming or for planting in similar waters which are unable to support the commoner types.

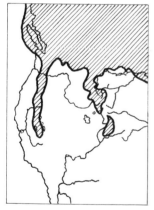

The Great Basin showing the southern extent of Wisconsin Period glaciation.

Rare Trout of North America

Most of the rare North American trout species are found in or around the Great Basin of the western US. Once a region of extensive inland seas, this area, between the Rocky Mountains and the coastal sierras, was inhabited by large populations of migratory cutthroat trout. As the seas shrank the remaining lake systems such as Pyramid, Walker, Malheur and Great Salt Lake each developed its own race of trout while populations no longer able to migrate became isolated in small headwater streams. It is to the primitive cutthroats of this region, as well as to some rainbow stocks of the western sierras, that the North American rare trouts are related; most are regarded as local races but a few have sufficient genetic differences to be classified as separate species.

Often described as the most exotically coloured of all trout, the **Californian Golden Trout (*S. aquabonita*)** is a prestige sporting fish of western North America. A native of the upper Kern River system in the Californian Sierras, it has been widely planted in other western states. Self-sustaining populations exist in Wyoming, Idaho, Washington and Alberta, although many have hybridised with cutthroat or rainbow trout. Goldens introduced to lowland waters tend to lose some of their distinctive colouring and are therefore stocked in mountain areas only.

Golden trout.

The nearest relative of the golden, and its possible ancestor, is believed to be the non-migratory race of rainbow trout once found in Kern river headwaters. Like other rare western trout, however, goldens also have genetic links with the cutthroat.

Fly fishing is the common angling technique for goldens in their native Sierras. Mainly small fish under 1 lb, their diet consists mainly of insects; wet flies, nymphs, dry flies or small hairwing patterns are all used to tempt them. They will also take natural baits and in lakes may respond readily to spinners.

The densely spotted, thickset **Apache trout (*S. apache*)** is native to the headwaters of Arizona's Salt River. At one time its range had shrunk to a few streams but pure-bred fish from the last stronghold on the Fort Apache Indian reservation were used in a programme of artificial enhancement. Fishing on the Fort Apache streams is restricted but a number of public waters are now stocked with this species.

A similar fish to the apache trout, but with more densely spotted dorsal and tail fins, the **Gila Trout (*S. gilae*)** is a native to high headwaters of the Gila River in New Mexico. A protected species in its few native creeks, it has been planted in a number of other western streams.

NORTH-AMERICAN SUBSPECIES Protein electrophoresis, which enables fine measurement of genetic variations, has shown that individual river systems, and even parts of the same stream, often hold genetically distinct forms of native species. Some are different enough in appearance to have been given local names and although most are regarded as races or subspecies the precise classification of some is impossible to determine.

Among cutthroat trout the coastal subspecies and the Yellowstone form are the most common; these and the once-widespread Lahontan cutthroat, which is uniquely adapted to the alkaline waters of the Great Basin, are discussed on page 79. Of the many less well-known races those which have been give subspecies status include the **Rio Grande cutthroat (*S.c. virginalis*),** the **green-backed trout (*S.c. stomias*),** the **Colorado cutthroat (*S.c. pleuriticus*),** the **Humboldt trout (*S.c. humboldtensis*)** and the **Bonneville cutthroat (*S.c. utah*).** These fish have distinctive colours and markings which are weakened or lost when the fish are planted in lowland waters.

There are fewer local forms of rainbow trout, probably because this species is more migratory in character and has had less opportunity to become isolated. The anadromous steelhead is usually seen as the definitive genotype of the species although several important freshwater forms occur. Best known is the Kamloops variety which, though relatively slow-growing and difficult to rear, is a useful fish for establishing resident populations in new river systems. Other important forms include the mountain Kamloops, the Oregon red banded, the Nelson, the Kern River, the Shasta and the Eagle Lake rainbow. Both the shasta form, from the McCloud river, and the Kern River one are now hybridised with introduced rainbows. Two other forms may also be virtually extinct, the little San Giorgiono trout of southern California and the Nelson trout of New Mexico.

The **Eagle Lake rainbow** has been given the subspecific name of ***S.g. aquilarium***. Eagle Lake is a big water lying at over 5,000 ft (1,500 metres) in the Lahontan Basin, home of several unusual varieties of trout. This subspecies has been known to reach eleven years, older than any other rainbow, and it has some cutthroat-like characteristics which have made its classification as a rainbow trout disputed. The gradual lowering of Eagle Lake has made access increasingly difficult to Pine Creek, its only spawning stream, and stocks are now enhanced by hatchery rearing. Eagle Lake rainbows have been planted in other waters in California's Lassen and Modoc Counties. Often running to a large size, they are esteemed sport fish in California.

Steelhead rainbows also have genetic variations in different river systems and in Asia a distinctive type, noted for its small size, is found in some streams tributary to the Sea of Okhotsk.

Eagle Lake rainbow trout

Rare Trout of Eurasia

Brown trout are usaully easy to recognise throughout their large natural range. There are however some distinctive local varieties which, like the North American rare trouts, are found along the margins of past glaciations. There are also several races of sea-run browns and the species is sometimes regarded as a composite one with many genetic types. The rare trouts of Eurasia are believed to be descended from the brown trout or, in a few cases, from extinct ancestral forms.

The sea trout of northern Europe is often regarded as the genotype of the species. The main subspecies are the **Caspian trout (*S.t. caspius*)**, sometimes called the Caspian salmon; the **Aral trout (*S.t. aralensis*)**, and the **Black Sea trout (*S.t. labrax*)**. The giant Caspian trout was was thought to be a species intermediate between brown trout and the Atlantic salmon until chromosome studies revealed that it had 60 chromosomes, the same as brown trout; Atlantic salmon have 80. It has a salmon-like life cycle and, like some European races, the Kura River form spawns only once. The Caspian trout has been severely reduced in numbers by the erection of dams on its spawning rivers; the Aral trout has also suffered from the huge irrigation schemes which are turning the shrinking Aral Sea into a salt lake.

Caspian trout individuals have been recorded in excess of 100 lbs

Few of the freshwater races found in the watersheds of these seas have been studied. Turkey has rare spotless trout and other forms occur in the Tigris and the Euphrates headwaters. Iran, which has the Caspian trout in the north, also has brown trout in Persian Gulf headstreams flowing out the Kurdistan ranges and an isolated subspecies (***S. macrostigmata***) is found in the mountains of Lebanon. Other distinct races are undoubtedly present on the Oxus

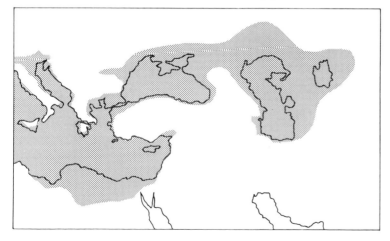

The Mediterranean, Black, Caspian and Aral seas are believed to have been joined in a single ancient sea which connected the Atlantic Ocean with Central Asia. Brown and sea trout populations thrive today in the separated watersheds.

slope of the Hindu Kush and Wakhan ranges of Afghanistan, in the Greater Pamir of Soviet Central Asia, and in the Caucasus mountains. The **Atlas trout (*S. pallaryi*)**, Africa's only native trout, may be close to extinction.

Several relict forms of European brown trout have been named as separate species. The **marbled trout (*S. marmoratus*)** of Yugoslavia is probably the best known. Strikingly marked and growing to 40 lbs, it is an important sporting fish. Adults are largely piscivorous and angling methods include large flies, spinners or natural fish baits. A native of the larger rivers of Dalmatia, the marbled trout now hybridises with introduced brown trout in some areas. Strict fishing limitations are in force to assist in its conservation.

Marbled trout.

The **softmouth trout (*S. obtusirostris*)** is another fish unique to Yugoslavia. It is similar in colour to the brown trout but has a distinctive small, underslung mouth and is sometimes classified in a separate genus, *Platysalmo*. The softmouth is native to the Neretva River and neighbouring watersheds; it can be taken on the fly and reaches weights up to 10 lbs.

In the Macedonian mountains of Greece and Yugoslavia there are several exotic species which could have links with pre-Pleistocene times over 100 milion years ago. Like the softmouth, three of them are sometimes placed in the genus *Platysalmo* – the **Ohrid trout (*P. ohridanus*)**, a riverine species (***P. zetensis***) and the **Montenegrin trout (*P. montenegris*)**. Four other *Salmo* subspecies also exist in Macedonia and the upper reaches of Greek streams in the Mediterranean Sea watershed.

The **Lake Garda trout (*S. carpio*)** of Italy is the best known of other southern forms inhabiting Alpine and Pyrennean streams. Northern Europe also has a number of unique forms most of which have probably developed since trout recolonised the area after the glacial retreat of 10,000 years ago. Ireland's Lough Melvin, a famous angling water, has three races, Gillaroo, Sonaghan and Ferox. They are distinct in appearance, in feeding ranges within the lough and in spawning areas, and electrophoretic studies have shown them to have genetic differences.

Scotland also has some rare forms. Genetic studies have raised the possibility of the famous Ferox trout of Highland char lochs being related to a primitive race of brown trout which entered Britain before the modern type; one group of lochs has a unique golden, densely speckled trout which may be a pure strain of this older race. A number of other lochs have forms with genetic rather than environmental differences and further electrophoretic tests can be expected to throw light on relationships between some of the races which occur both in the British Isles and on the European mainland.

Sea-going trout have a number of European races in addition to the Asian subspecies. The Baltic race grows to an exceptional size in the brackish waters of that sea; in Finland it has been recorded to 46½ lbs and Sweden's famous Morrum River has produced many fish over 20 lbs.

A unique strain of sea trout is found in some north-eastern British rivers, notably the Tweed. Like the Caspian race it has a salmon-like life history, running to sea for a number of years, returning at a large size and tending to spawn only once. These fish travel the North Sea as far as Norway and it has been suggested that they are the remnant of an ancient Rhine race perhaps rivalling the Caspian trout in size. The North Sea, which is reckoned to be the world's most productive fishing ground, was a great river before the English Channel appeared only a few thousand years ago. Sea trout are known to thrive in brackish seas and the waters off the ancient Rhine, into which most north European rivers flowed, would have comprised a major feeding area of this type.

Today Tweed sea trout average over 5 lbs and fish of 15–20 lbs are taken regularly; unfortunately for the angler they are hard to catch and are often taken by fishermen after salmon. Other main races of the sea trout in the British Isles have been linked to ancient systems – the Irish Sea river and the English Channel river. Streams facing the open Atlantic Ocean also have recognisable types and those from the west coast of Ireland grow more slowly, especially during their post-smolt stage, than sea trout from other areas of the British Isles.

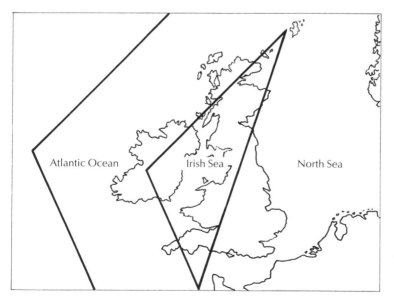

Feeding grounds of British sea trout. Atlantic stocks have a slower growth rate than those of the Irish and North Seas.

HYBRIDS

The close relationship between salmon, trout and char is demonstrated by the fact that in hatcheries virtually any of them can be crossed to produce hybrids. The many experiments which have been made in this field have, however, shown great variability in the ratios of eggs or fry which develop successfully. Hybrids often grow well but many, especially inter-generic ones, remain infertile. The fact that these infertile fish often use the energy which would have been used in egg and milt production into added growth makes some of them of interest to trout farmers as table fish.

The appearance of the splake is intermediate to that of its parent lake and brook trout.

The wendigo or splake is a cross between two chars, the brook trout and the lake trout. First used in Canada for planting as a sporting fish, it has been stocked in many Ontario lakes and has proved a popular angling fish; it has also been planted in a number of other waters in the Great Lakes area and elsewhere. This cross is fertile.

Another hybrid which is occasionally stocked for angling is the exotically marked tiger trout, an inter-generic cross between the brown trout (*Salmo*) and the brook trout (*Salvelinus*); it is infertile. Tiger trout have been known to occur in the wild; such inter-generic crosses are, however, extremely rare and crosses between members of the same genus are also rare under natural conditions. The rainbow-cutthroat group does so, however, in some areas. Though these two species breed separately over most of their range, genetically mixed hatchery strains may interbreed freely; both also hybridise with most of the rare trouts of the Great Basin.

Atlantic salmon and brown trout may also hybridise in the wild. Though crosses are uncommon they occur regularly enough to be of significance in the correct identification of record-class fish. Though they can sometimes be identified by eye, genetic tests are the only way of knowing for certain whether, for instance, a very large sea trout is a hybrid or not; a recent fish from the Tweed weighing 28½ lbs turned out to be a pure sea trout.

Brown trout also cross in nature with some of the rare south European and Middle Eastern trouts if they have access to them. Rare species as well as important local forms of salmonids are easily destroyed by crossing with their more common relatives and, in order to conserve these unique fish, organisations responsible for stocking natural waters should restrict introductions wherever possible to native fish from the same stream.

6 THE CHARS, TAIMEN AND HUCHEN

Chars are the dominant salmonids of cold northern waters. They occur both as freshwater residents and as sea-run fish in Arctic and subarctic regions, and as purely freshwater forms in cool montane waters of the temperate zone. They occupy similar habitats to trout and their superficially similar appearance has led to some of them being commonly called trouts.

The most widely known of the chars is the brook trout. A major gamefish of eastern North America – which has no native true trout – it has been introduced to angling waters in several parts of the world. Another North American species, the lake trout, has been less widely planted outside its native range but has become widely known for its large size. The important Arctic char is unique among the salmonids in its cicumpolar distribution, being a common fish in far northern parts of Europe, Asia and North America. The other major species, the Dolly Varden and east Asian chars, are closely related to the Arctic char but have a more southerly distribution and are limited to the Pacific basin. In addition there are numerous local forms of char derived from one of the four principal species which exist as ice-age relics isolated in cold upland lakes both in North America and Eurasia.

Wild char are relatively slow-growing fish. The summer growing period in their typical northern habitats is too short to allow for great seasonal weight gains. Most have a long life span, however, and some reach very large sizes by sustained growth over ten or more years. In Arctic regions they are important to local subsistence fisheries and some support commercial operations. All are recognized sporting fish and in some areas they are the mainstay of sporting fisheries.

With the exception of the brook trout char populations have remained in a healthier state than those of trout and salmon. Although increasingly threatened by acid rain the vast wilderness areas of northern Canada and Siberia have not suffered the degree of habitat degradation that have afflicted industrial regions to the south. Char stocks, however, are very vulnerable to exploitation, especially in far northern waters where even angling pressure can have a long-term effect.

Another important salmonid group consists of the charlike huchens of Eurasia. The principal member is the taimen, which reaches a larger size than any other salmonid. Abundant in the rivers of Siberia its habitat, like that of the closely related Danubian huchen, is restricted entirely to fresh water.

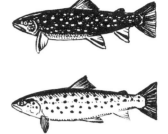

Char can be told apart from trout and salmon by the light markings on a dark background (top). These markings show up best at the low light intensities which typify char habitats for much of the year. Trout and salmon have the opposite arrangement – dark markings on a lighter background.

Brook Trout

JUVENILES

1 Parr   These can be distinguished from those of the true trouts by the light spots on a dark background. The parr marks are long and straight-sided, their thickness greater than the spaces between.

ADULTS

2 Small female   Brook trout from small streams commonly retain the juvenile parr marks. They can be told apart from other char by the wavy vermiculated lines on the back and the dark markings on dorsal fin and tail; from salmon and true trouts by the pale markings on a dark background. Most also have very small red spots with blue halos similar to those of brown trout. The lower fins are red or orange with contrasting black-and-white leading edges.

3 Large female   The general markings (above) are distinct although colouring may vary with habitat. The large mouth is characteristic; the upper jaw of both sexes extends well beyond the rear of the eye.

4 Male in breeding dress   The exotic colours are hard to mistake. A black line normally develops on the lower flanks separating the red area from the white belly; the snout becomes elongated, the lower jaw develops a small hook and the shoulder acquires a moderate hump.

5 Sea-run brook trout in ocean dress   Rarely exceeding four lbs in weight, it can be distinguished from small Atlantic salmon grilse by the long upper jaw, square tail and thick tail stalk. The silvery flanks fade rapidly and after 2 or 3 weeks in the river anadromous brook trout become practically indistinguishable from freshwater residents.

Note: All species of char can be distinguished from trout and salmon by the pale body spots (no dark ones) and the tiny, almost indistinguishable scales. Their dentition differs from trout; there are teeth at the tip of the vomer bone on the roof of the mouth while trout have teeth along the shaft of the vomer as well. Chars also have relatively soft bodies with thin stomach walls, the muscle bands on which are clearly defined. They also have rather large fins.

FINRAY AND SCALE COUNTS There are normally 10 rays in the dorsal fin and 9 in the anal fin. The scales are too small to be easily counted.

FLIES From left: Montreal, Professor, Scarlet Ibis, Yellow Sally, Parmachene Belle, Woolly Worm (wet flies); Royal Coachman hairwing (dry fly); Grizzly King Streamer (streamer fly).

PLATE XI

1
2
3
4
5

Lake Trout

1 Adult male   The lake trout has a relatively standard appearance with few local forms. The strongly forked tail distinguishes it from most other adult trout and char, including the hybrid splake. The body is generally a dull grey-green or grey-blue with numerous pale yellowish spots on the head, body dorsal fin and tail. At breeding time the body may turn a rusty shade with reddish, white-edged lower fins. A characteristic feature is the raised tooth crest at the head of the vomer bone.

Arctic Char

2 Sea-run female in ocean dress   The flanks are silvery with large, pale spots.
3 Sea-run male in breeding dress   The brilliant red or orange flanks are also common on male lake-dwelling arctic char at spawning time.
4 Pelagic lake form in summer dress   Isolated races differ in details but most are small fish with deeply forked tails and small mouths.
5 Benthic lake form   This dwarf type is often found in the same lakes as the pelagic form.
Note: Arctic char can be distinguished from the similar brook trout by the lack of markings on dorsal fin and tail; red spots, when present, lack blue halos.

Dolly Varden

6 Closely resembling the related Arctic char, dolly varden can be distinguished by their smaller spots, the largest of which do not normally exceed the diameter of the eye. In northern areas some individuals have slight vermiculations on the back. Dolly varden have a similar range of forms to the Arctic char including large sea-run and lake-dwelling forms and dwarf freshwater types.

East Asian Char

7 Japanese landlocked form   Isolated freshwater races vary in appearance but the large spots and small vermiculations are common. Large sea-run individuals closely resemble anadromous Arctic char and dolly varden.

Taimen and Huchen

8 Adult male taimen   The body is long and cylindrical, the head flat and the mouth very large. The small, dark spots are restricted to the head and body. At spawning time the coppery tinge on the flanks deepens and often extends over the body. Taimen are distinguished from the similar huchen by the smaller number of gillrakers on the first arch; 11 or 12 compared to 16 for the huchen.

PLATE XII

```
         1
         2
         3
    4        5
         6
         7
         8
```

91

BROOK TROUT

Salvelinus fontinalis

Names

The common name derives from the typical small-stream habitat. Other names include eastern brook trout, speckled trout and native trout. Sea-run brook trout are known locally as salters or sea trout. 'Fontinalis' means 'living in springs'. Local races and subspecies are often named separately, e.g. aurora trout and Dublin pond char.

Distribution

The native range of the brook trout is eastern North America from the Hudson Straits south to the mountain streams of Georgia and the Carolinas. It was once a common fish as far west as some of the headwaters of the Mississippi and in the Lake Superior watershed but is now absent from many areas; its centre of abundance today is in the Canadian provinces of Manitoba, Quebec, Ontario and Newfoundland. Anadromous brook trout enter coastal streams from the Hudson Straits to Maine.

Naturalised populations of brook trout occur in many parts of the western US and Canada, in Chile and Argentina, Australia and New Zealand, and in some European countries.

Size

In small streams brook trout often mature at under 6 inches (15 cm) and may never grow much larger. Northern rivers and lakes, however, commonly produce fish exceeding 1 lb in weight. Prime waters in Canada, South America and New Zealand are known for the occasional specimen of 10 lbs or more; the angling record of 14½ lbs was caught by Dr W.J. Cook from the Nipigon river, Ontario in 1916.

Sea-run brook trout enter rivers and streams at an average weight of about 1 lb. Their individual size varies from immature specimens of under ½ lb to adults of 5 or 6 lbs.

Exploitation

An excellent eating fish, the brook trout was once the subject of commercial fishing in eastern North America but today it is conserved as a sporting species. Exotically coloured and a free taker to angling lures it is the most important gamefish in parts of its native range where it is still common.

Though rarely favoured by trout farmers as a food fish, due to its slow growth rate compared to rainbow trout, the brook trout is reared in many parts of the world to stock angling waters.

Life Cycle

Young brook trout hatch out and emerge from the spawning gravels of streams, rivers and lakes during spring. Their growth rate under good conditions is similar to those of the true trouts and faster than most other chars. Where ideal water temperatures are maintained year-round they can attain 3 or 4 lbs in three years. More typically, they grow slowly, often attaining three inches (7½ cm) in length or less during their first growing season in streams. Brook trout also have a relatively short life expectancy compared to other chars. Although individuals have been known to live to over 20, in southern areas few live longer than four or five years.

Caddis larvae are a staple for trout in small streams.

Brook trout spend most of their time in the slower stretches of streams and rivers. Their early diet in small streams consists largely of insects with caddis larvae often comprising a significant proportion. They are voracious feeders, however, and will take most available food items including other fish. While often feeding well during daytime they tend like most salmonids to be most active in early morning and late evening, and while they will feed to some extent at near-freezing temperatures their optimum range is 12–15°C (54–60°F). This temperature range is much the same as the feeding optimum for the true trouts, but their upper tolerance level is less and brook trout are unlikely to survive for long above 20°C (69°F).

Most brook trout leave the parent headwaters to seek better feeding areas downstream before returning again to spawn in the autumn. Typical spawning sites are small, cold springheads but suitable rivers as well as the wave-washed shores of lakes are also used. Chars have a stronger tendency to spawn in lakes than trout and this characteristic has encouraged the establishment of self-sustaining populations of brook trout in mountain lakes in several parts of the world.

Brook trout mature early, the males often being sexually developed by the end of their first year and the females by the end of their second. As the spawning period approaches their body colours strengthen and the cock fish in breeding dress is often regarded as the most exotically attired of all the salmonids. The breeding ritual of the brook trout follows the usual salmonid pattern but like other chars they appear to suffer less physical stress from spawning than trout or salmon and the male can provide good sport and good eating right after spawning.

Angling

The early traditions of North American sport fishing were centred around brook trout and the cold, clear streams of New England. British settlers were successful in taking the brook trout by their traditional methods, including fly fishing which at that time was a relatively undeveloped practice. British innovations continued to influence American angling but the distinctive character of the fish and the new types of water soon led to the development of indigenous methods. The bright new brook trout flies which joined such venerable patterns as the March Brown foreshadowed the many later developments in tackle and technique.

March Brown. Popular on both sides of the Atlantic, this pattern is probably the oldest still in common use.

Although the brook trout has a superficial resemblance to the brown trout its feeding behaviour is distinctly different. In clear water it will often accept large offerings – flies, spinners or natural baits – which the brown will rarely take except under cover of darkness or of flood water. The brookie in fact is much easier to catch; in a controlled experiment five were caught to every brown trout. Its relative lack of awareness does not mean that it is always easy to tempt. It has the same excellent eyesight as other salmonids and regular success, particularly with the big ones, relies both on a cautious approach and a sound knowledge of its feeding patterns.

STREAM AND RIVER FISHING Typical brook trout haunts in running water are sheltered spots away from heavy currents including pools, undercut banks, behind rocks or beneath timber deadfalls. Small fish can usually be tempted from such places during daytime but the big ones often respond better at dawn and dusk or during periods of high water when they feed heavily on food items washed down with the flood.

The standard trout fishing methods will all take brookies and a choice can be made according to individual preference or the character of a particular stream. Heavy tackle is unnecessary except where the fish run unusually large or the water is snag-ridden. Brookies are lively fighters but on small streams average only a few ounces, except in autumn when on some waters spawning runs of bigger fish may arrive from larger waters downstream.

LAKE FISHING In shallow lakes brookies can be located in areas associated with good feeding such as the mouths of feeder streams, along the margins of the windward shore, around weed beds, in areas where aquatic insects are hatching, or where terrestrial insects are reaching the water from bankside trees. In deep lakes they can be more difficult to find especially in summer when they seek the depths to escape the heated upper layer. In thermally stratified lakes a thermometer can be used to locate the thermocline level along which they feed; a spinner or spoon can then be trolled at this depth.

Status

The relatively delicate balance of environmental conditions required by the brook trout has been widely disturbed by the activities of modern man. The first cause of its demise came in the southern parts of its range when large-scale deforestation in eastern North America led to water temperatures rising beyond the tolerance of the fish. Many more rivers were also destroyed by water pollution, abstraction, the building of dams and the introduction of foreign competitors in the form of brown and rainbow trout. The record-producing Nipigon, once the world's finest brook trout fishery with fish averaging several pounds, was degraded by a dam downstream which interfered with the trouts' passage to their Lake Superior feeding grounds. Today there is a serious problem from acid rain in some of the brook trout's other Canadian strongholds.

While environmental conservation is now partly a public political issue, stocking policy is a matter for anglers and fisheries organisations. The inappropriate introductions of non-native trout have in the past been exacerbated by the planting of poor strains of the brook trout itself; hatchery trout of mixed genetic background have been shown to grow more slowly and to survive less well in the wild than native strains. A positive move, and one which is now increasingly being applied to other salmonid fish, is the practice of restocking only with wild local fish which have a maximum chance of sustaining themselves.

In southern habitats the wild brook trout has for the most part retreated into Appalachian headwater streams where large populations of small fish still thrive. In New England it survives in similar remote streams while Maine and the Adirondacks have larger waters producing fish to several pounds. Farther west, scattered native populations are found into Michigan and the Lake Superior drainage area.

In Canada the brook trout is still abundant with the subarctic rivers flowing into Hudson's Bay being especially renowned for quality fishing; Manitoba, Ontario and Quebec regularly produce fish of 5–10 lb. In the Maritime Provinces some coastal streams also have substantial runs of sea-run brook trout.

In western North America the brook trout has been widely introduced with the Rocky Mountain states having many self-sustaining populations. Planted fish have also succeeded in establishing themselves in other parts of the world, most notably in the southern hemisphere. Patagonia has brook trout fishing rivalling that of the best Canadian waters. Europe has had less success with naturalised fish although brook trout are sometimes planted for put-and-take fishing.

LAKE TROUT

Salvelinus namaycush

Names
The common name comes from the stillwater habitat to which southern populations of this char are restricted. Other names include lake char, mackinaw, grey trout and togue. 'Namaycush' is an Indian word.

Distribution

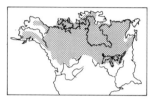

The lake trout is a native of North America, its range being almost entirely confined to freshwater habitats within the areas of Pleistocene glaciation. It is found in the basin of the Great Lakes and parts of New England, in most of the Atlantic and Hudson's Bay drainage areas of Canada and in the entire Arctic watershed including several islands in the northern archipelago. In the west it occurs naturally in some Missouri headwater areas, in the upper reaches of the Fraser and in other British Columbia watersheds from the Skeena northwards, while in Alaska it is found in southern drainages up to the Susitna river, in the Bristol Bay drainage, the upper Yukon and the Brooks Range.

The lake trout has been widely introduced in parts of North America outside its natural range, most notably in Rocky Mountain lakes. It has occasionally been planted in other parts of the world.

Size
One of the largest salmonid fishes, the lake trout averages several pounds in weight and often exceeds 10 lbs. In prime Canadian lakes 30–40 lb fish are taken regularly; the angling record, caught on Great Bear Lake in the Northwest Territories in 1970 weighed 65 lbs. Commercially caught lake trout include one from Lake Athabaska in Saskatchewan weighing 102 lbs.

Exploitation
The lake trout is an important sport fish in southern parts of its range and many anglers fly north in search of trophy-sized specimens from the wilderness lakes of Canada. Its good eating qualities, large size and widespread distribution also make it an attractive commercial species. The Great Lakes supported a major net fishery before the demise of their lake trout stocks and big northern waters such as Great Slave Lake still operate important fisheries; in northern Canada it is the second most important commercial species after the whitefishes.

The slow growth of the lake trout has not encouraged fish farmers to rear it for food but it is raised in some North American hatcheries for stocking angling waters.

Life Cycle

The fry of the lake trout move rapidly down into deep water after springtime emergence from the spawning beds. Their early growth relies on an invertebrate diet and the Arctic freshwater shrimp, *Mysis relicta*, is known to be particularly important. Later they feed heavily on other fish, taking whatever species is available; whitefish, ciscoes and sticklebacks are common fare in northern lakes. In the numerous small lakes on the Barren Grounds, where lake trout are often the only species present, they will feed readily on their own kind.

Round whitefish, a staple for lake trout in many northern areas.

Though often regarded as a purely lake-dwelling fish the lake trout is also found in rivers in the northern parts of its range. In the Arctic it is one of the commonest species in shallow river and lake systems, often living in association with Arctic char, brook trout, Arctic grayling or the northern pike which it commonly exceeds in size. It hunts wherever the water is cool enough and prey can be found; one from the Great Bear Lake was captured while feeding on *Mysis* shrimps at a depth of 1,400 ft (425 metres).

Growth rates are slow but vary considerably according to latitude. In Great Slave Lake a 5 lb fish is often found to be around ten years old and a 20 lb fish 20 years old. In Great Bear Lake further north growth rates are considerably slower. Maturity is usually reached at between five and eleven years and life expectancy is very long – lake trout are believed to have reached at least 50 years in age.

Lake trout are physically adapted to eating huge amounts of food during the short Arctic growing season. The distended stomach is a common feature on northern lakes in summer.

Spawning takes place in lakes except in a few southern areas where it may occur in deep rivers. The spawning time varies from September in the far north to late December in the Great Lakes region. The breeding dress of the lake trout is less pronounced than that of other chars, the typical grey-green or brownish body colours turning to rusty brown with reddish, white-edged fins.

Spawning sites in lakes are located in rocky areas, sometimes in the marginal shallows but occasionally as deep as 100 ft (30 metres). The lake trout is unusual among the salmonids in that nest-building is dispensed with, the site merely being swept by the hen fish before eggs are deposited. The number of eggs laid is relatively low and predation from other fish heavy but lake trout populations do not appear to suffer from these apparent drawbacks.

Angling

Lake trout can be caught in shallow waters by standard trout-fishing methods but in deep lakes they are most commonly sought by specialised trolling tactics.

Successful deep-water trolling depends on the skilful use of relatively heavy gear. The metal lines made specially for the purpose are best; in very deep water they provide a sensitivity impossible to achieve with springy nylon lines. In big lakes 400–500 ft (120–150 metres) of metal line with a similar length of nylon backing is commonly used in combination with a large-diameter centrepin or standard sea fishing reel and a short, stout trolling rod with overall action but enough sensitivity at the top end to work the bait.

Typical end tackle includes a big spoon on a heavy nylon leader attached to the main line by a three-way swivel. On the bottom link of the swivel a short link is attached to a weight heavy enough to keep the spoon working near the lake bed. Alternatively the lead can be fixed above the spoon and between the two a big vibrating flasher in the manner of Pacific salmon trolling. If the flasher is used it can pay to work the line by pulling the rod back and forth to give added action to the spoon, while taking care to avoid wear on the line at the rod tip by reeling in a little at intervals.

In this type of fishing a skilled guide or companion is an obvious asset in locating fishing grounds, handling the boat or netting the fish.

Although deep trolling is the standard way of taking lake trout they can sometimes be caught on light trolling gear, or by spinning, at dawn and dusk off deep-water shorelines. Like other salmonids they tend to be most active at these times and will make brief forays into the warmer surface layers. They will also take spinner or bait in certain locations in autumn, when they come in to spawn, or for a brief period on early spring before surface waters become too heated.

In northern Canada the lake trout can be caught all season in shallow lakes and rivers on big bucktails and streamers or by spinning. Fishing camps served by float plane cater for anglers in search of lake trout and other chars of the northern wilderness areas.

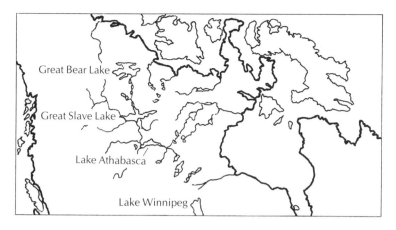

Lake trout country.

Status

In Canada, which contains a quarter of the world's fresh waters, the lake trout remains a common and widely distributed fish. In the largest lakes such as Athabaska, Great Slave and Great Bear they have been exploited by man for many years but countless smaller waters remain to be opened up to fishing. In southern Canada and the northern US the lake trout has lost important habitats. The Great Lakes once comprised the single most important fishery for lake trout prior to their virtual extinction by sea lampreys accidentally introduced after the construction of the Welland Canal between Lake Ontario and Lake Erie. Before this disaster the Lake had also supported a sporting fishery, the largest lake trout caught on rod and line being a 63—pounder from Lake Superior in 1952. Today Pacific salmon and rainbow trout have been successfully established in the Lakes while the lake trout has become a marginal species in the area.

In its prime Canadian habitats the main angling pressure on the fish is centred on the very large specimens which are its main sporting attraction. Since angling methods commonly concentrate on taking trophy trout of 30 lbs and over even big lakes have proved vulnerable to over-exploitation by rod and line. Lake trout of this size are mostly over 20 years old and in order to maintain them in numbers a sustained yield policy is beneficial both to visitors and local interests. Fishery zoning is one approach which has been tried, with waters being specifically designated either for sporting or commercial use. Catch-and-release is encouraged and, while catch limits are mandatory, maximum and minimum size limits have also been proposed. This would mean the release of fish from 15 to 30 lbs and the removal of smaller ones, leaving more food available to speed the growth of the desirable 15 lb-plus category while allowing anglers to keep the major trophies over 30 lbs.

Introduction of lake trout outside their historic range has resulted in a number of self-sustaining populations in cold New England lakes, parts of the Mid-West and in many western areas. It has been planted in a few areas outside North America, notably in Sweden and Switzerland where naturalised populations now exist.

ARCTIC CHAR

Salvelinus alpinus

Name
The common name derives from the classic Arctic habitat; the Latin name means 'alpine'. Local forms may be known by separate names, e.g. Oquassa trout.

Distribution

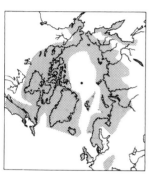

The unique circumpolar range of the Arctic char overlaps that of every other major species of trout, salmon and char. Sea-run Arctic char are abundant along the coast of northern Canada, Siberia, Lapland, Iceland and Greenland. Freshwater residents also occur in these regions as well as montane areas further south. Landlocked forms are found from eastern Asia west through Siberia and Europe including the Alps, Scandinavia and the British Isles, and in North America south to New England. These southern populations are believed to be relicts of the big char populations inhabiting these areas prior to the retreat of ice-age glaciers 10,000 years ago.

Size
Sea-run Arctic char commonly reach large sizes and on Canadian and Siberian rivers can average around 8 lbs with occasional specimens of 15–20 lbs or more. Sizes often go unrecorded but a fish of 33 lbs has been reported from Siberia and one of 29 lbs 11oz was angled from the Tree River in Canada's Northwest Territories in 1968.

Freshwater forms of Arctic char vary from dwarf types which never exceed a few ounces to deep-water piscivorous forms which can attain similar weights to sea-run fish. Relict populations in more southerly areas commonly consist of small fish under 1 lb.

Exploitation
The Arctic char has long been of major importance as a quality food fish to northern peoples such as the North American Inuit, the Sami of Lapland and the Yakut of Siberia. Small-scale subsistence fisheries operate for sea-run char on many Arctic coasts as well as a number of larger operations, notably in the USSR where the Arctic char is an important commercial species.

As a sporting fish it is increasingly popular, especially in Canada, as more anglers fly north after the big sea-run char. Landlocked char are also important sport fish in waters where they attain large sizes.

Life Cycle

Most sea-run char spawn in autumn but some lakes hold separate populations of both spring and autumn spawners. After their emergence from the gravel sea-run fish spend up to a month as yolk-sac alevins before starting to feed. From the fry stage onwards their growth rate is very variable; in Icelandic rivers many run to sea at 6–8 inches (15–20 cm) after only one year's growth, in some Siberian rivers after two or three years, and in Arctic Canada they commonly migrate after five or six years in rivers, lakes or estuaries. Their age at maturity varies from about 3 to 12 years. In north-eastern Canada Arctic char have been known to live for as long as 25 years but take from 10 to 15 years to reach 5 lb in weight.

In the ocean char travel in shoals close to the shorelines, feeding on a diet similar to that of trout and salmon. Crustaceans, sand lance or sandeels, and capelin are typical food items and in some Siberian waters young cod are known to be a staple. Their stay in salt water is relatively short since they do not enter it until the ice melts in May or June and the whole population returns to fresh water from mid-July to October before the sea freezes again.

Spawning migrations are relatively short, most char spawning in the lower reaches of river systems in pools below falls or in lakes. Fresh-run fish are silvery sided with blue backs but as the breeding time approaches the lower parts turn red. The colour of the males is often striking, their dark blue-black backs contrasting strongly with intense red flanks and china-white leading edges of the lower fins. After spawning is completed these males commonly remain to guard the nests for days or weeks.

Lake-dwelling char populations are often characterised by the presence of two or three quite separate forms. Typically these consist of a large-headed dwarf type, an elegant, small-headed pelagic form and rarer big, deep-water type. The plasticity of the Arctic char is shown by the fact that most of these forms have probably developed their genetically distinct characters since the last ice age. They spawn either in tributary streams or along the lake shores, and the separation of breeding areas and times ensures that different forms maintain the genetic distinctions which help them maximise the potential of different environments within the same lake.

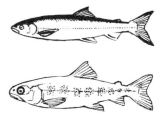

Separate forms of Arctic char occurring in the same lake can be very different in appearance.

Angling

Angling for sea-run char is concentrated on the lower reaches of rivers as the fish return from the sea. On most Arctic rivers they begin running in the second half of July with the best fishing continuing through the months of August and September.

These fish will feed in fresh water and once located are rarely difficult to tempt on artificial or natural baits. Big, bright bucktail and streamer flies are favourites while spoons, spinners and plugs will all take fish. All baits should be retrieved slowly and close to the river bed since char tend to take best near the bottom even in shallow water. They commonly follow for a long distance before taking and when hooked make fast, line-stripping runs.

Freshwater forms of Arctic char are also free takers but the small types are often plankton feeders requiring appropriately small baits. In cold northern lakes they can often be caught in shallow water but in lakes which heat up in summer both the small forms and the rarer large ones are most likely to be taken by trolling around the thermocline level.

All forms of Arctic char are highly regarded as food. In Arctic subsistence fisheries they are taken by a variety of small-scale methods similar to those which were once widely employed for trout and salmon. In the sea small gill nets, fish wheels and set lines are used along the shorelines in summer while returning fish are caught in small river traps and nets. An important method among the Inuit is based on the male char's habit of remaining at the spawning site; these are taken through the ice either by spearing or on jigs and baits.

Status

Most coastal rivers in Arctic regions have substantial runs of migratory arctic char. They are abundant in the Northwest Territories of Canada as far north as Ellesmere Island, in Greenland, the northern rivers of Iceland, the Arctic shores of Alaska, along the length of the Siberian coast and in northern Finland, Norway and Sweden.

The value of sea-run char as a sporting fish as well as a traditional subsistence species has led to increasing efforts towards efficient management of sea-run stocks. The very slow growth rate of most stocks means that wilderness waters which gain a reputation for good fishing can be hit hard by intensive angling; in Canada there is a trend towards maintaining important fisheries on a sustained yield basis with restrictions on both types of fishing. There is sufficient water in the Canadian Arctic to retain good stocks for visiting anglers without affecting the rights of subsistence fishers.

Ice fishing.

DOLLY VARDEN

Salvelinus malma

Name
The common name has been credited to scientists working on California's McCloud River. Women members of the party likened the appearance of the fish to a fashionable spotted print cloth of the period, called dolly varden after a character in the Dickens novel Barnaby Rudge. The Latin name is from a local term in Kamchatka.

Distribution
In North America the dolly varden is found on the Pacific slope from the McCloud River north to the Bering Straits and in Asia from the Anadyr river south to Hokkaido and to the Yalu in Korea. In North America isolated populations also occur east of the continental divide in the Liard, Peace and Athabasca systems of northern Canada. Sea-run dolly varden occur in many coastal rivers.

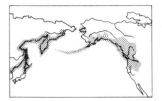

Size
Sea-run dolly varden commonly average several pounds in weight while dwarf forms common in some northern lakes never exceed a few ounces. In southern areas freshwater forms often reach large sizes; one of 40 lb 2oz was reported from British Columbia's Lardeau river, and angling records include a fish of 35 lb from the Duncan river in the same province and one of 32 lb from Idaho.

Exploitation
In North America the dolly varden is of little commercial interest but enjoys local status as a sporting species. It is an excellent eating fish.

Life Cycle
The biology of the dolly varden is similar to that of its close relative, the Arctic char. It has a reputation as a heavy predator on eggs and fry of the Pacific salmon but studies have indicated that dolly varden are probably no worse in this respect than trout.

Angling
Although the dolly is a popular rod species in some areas it is overshadowed by the salmon, steelhead or rainbow trout which share its waters. In lakes it tends to put up a slow fight but sea-run fish are game, making the same sort of long, powerful runs as migratory Arctic char. It is not difficult to tempt and can be taken on a fly, spinner or bait in rivers and lake margins and, in deep waters, by trolling.

East Asian Char (*Salvelinus leucomaenis*)
Like the dolly varden, the East Asian char is another member of the Arctic char group which is commonly classified as a separate species. Japan has many localised fresh-water forms of this fish. The large basin of the Sea of Okhotsk has all three major forms – the dolly varden, the East Asian char and the Arctic char itself.

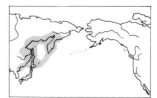

TAIMEN

Hucho taimen

The taimen is a charlike fish which parallels the North American lake trout in its large size and widespread distribution in northern fresh waters.

Name

Taimen is the common Siberian name. In Finland and the western USSR the same name is applied to brown trout.

Distribution

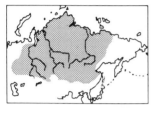

The taimen is found in rivers and lakes throughout much of northern Asia. It occurs as far west as the middle reaches of the Volga and in Siberia it is found in all rivers from the Pechora east to the Kolyma basin, and the southern watersheds of the Sea of Okhotsk. The southern boundary is from the upper Ural river through northern Kazakhstan, central Mongolia and north-west China.

Size

The largest living salmonid, the taimen is the only species which may reach 200 lbs. In big rivers such as the Yenisey and Amur it regularly reaches 100 lbs and individuals have been known to 185 lbs. The average size taken by fishermen is probably 10–20 lbs.

Exploitation

A locally important commercial species, the taimen is taken in small-scale net fisheries in many regions. It is highly regarded as a sport fish and it is sought by similar methods to those used to catch its close relative, the Danubian huchen. The taimen is a major freshwater predator; it is not normally taken on fly but responds well to natural baits and spinners which imitate the local forage fish.

Life Cycle

Taimen head showing broad maxillary.

The fry of taimen emerge from the gravel in the late spring and usually reach 5 or 6 inches (13–15 cm) by the end of their first year. Most migrate from spawning streams into nearby lakes and rivers; the classic taimen habitat is in deep water adjoining fast reaches of big mountain rivers. Young fish quickly become piscivorous and grow increasingly fast with age. Its lifespan sometimes exceeds fifteen years.

Taimen breed in spring, usually April, their preferred spawning grounds being in small streams and the gravelly reaches of some rivers. Prior to spawning both sexes become darker in appearance, their bodies commonly turning a deep copper red. This colour is most noticeable among the male fish which also develop a hooked lower jaw. The spawning sequence follows the usual salmonid pattern and the eggs usually develop and hatch within six weeks. Like char, the taimen mends well after spawning and mortality is low.

DANUBIAN HUCHEN

Hucho hucho

Differing from it in minor respects only, the huchen is now regarded as a local race of the more widely distributed taimen.

Name
Huchen is the central European term.

Distribution
The natural range is limited to the Danube basin including parts of southern Germany, Austria, Yugoslavia, Czechoslovakia and Romania. It is restricted mainly to the middle and upper reaches of the main river and its tributaries; it never visits the Black Sea but enters some lower reaches of the Danube to spawn.

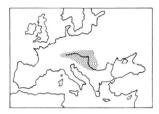

Size
Most rod-caught huchen are between 5 and 20 lbs. Like the taimen it may reach a very large size and individuals have been recorded in excess of 100 lbs.

Exploitation
A prestigious sporting fish, the huchen is now conserved for angling on most of its waters. It is mainly fished for over the winter months and is taken on large spoons and spinners as well as natural baits such as the nase, its principal prey. The huchen is a very powerful fish requiring strong tackle; though it rarely leaps when hooked it makes long, very fast runs and has great stamina.

A combination of habitat loss and over-fishing has resulted in the huchen becoming rare in many of its native waters. Some fisheries have been closed for periods up to several years to conserve stocks and on others there are strict limitations on open seasons or on the size and number of fish which may be killed.

The nase.

Life Cycle
The habitats and life history of the Danubian huchen are similar to those of the taimen.

East Asian Huchens
There are at least two forms of East Asian huchen which, like the Danubian form, have been given different specific names from the related taimen. One Asian form – *H. perryi* – is unique among the group in that it runs to sea, entering the northern half of the Sea of Japan and spawning in the adjacent rivers of the Sikhote Alin mountains, Sakhalin and Hokkaido. Like its freshwater-resident relatives it may reach a large size; it differs from them physically in a number of respects including minor details of dentition and its larger scales. Another East Asian huchen – *H. ischikawa* – is restricted to a small area in the highlands of North Korea and southern Manchuria.

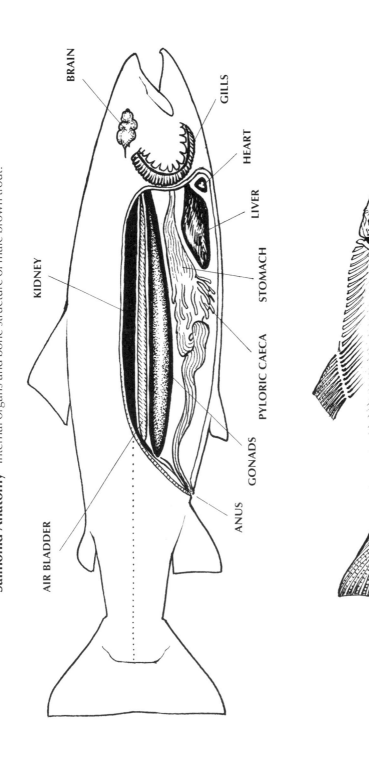

Salmonid Anatomy Internal organs and bone structure of male brown trout.

BRAIN

GILLS

HEART

LIVER

STOMACH

PYLORIC CAECA

GONADS

ANUS

AIR BLADDER

KIDNEY

ANATOMY

The classic streamlined body shape of salmon, trout and char reflects their nature as high energy-swimmers. They move by undulating the whole body, with fins acting largely as rudders and stabilisers. Normal swimming is effected through the heavy musculature which accounts for most of the body weight while high-speed movement is enhanced by the bands of red muscle along the lateral line area.

As sight hunters, their eyes are particularly significant. Controlled by the optic lobes which form the largest part of the salmonid brain, they are capable of reacting to visual stimuli many times faster than humans. Colour perception is acute and many species have good night vision. The eyes also control changes in skin colour.

Other senses include internal ears, concerned mainly with balance; taste buds located in the mouth; and nostrils which are capable of distinguishing certain smells at concentrations of a few parts per million. The sensitive lateral line, which extends onto the head as a series of pores, is an extension of the nervous system and is used to detect water vibrations.

Colours and markings are related to both camouflage and communication. The camouflage aspect is reflected by the ability to quickly match the shade of the substrate when seen from above; by dazzling silver flanks among the sea-run fish; and by a light belly, the scales of which are shaped to deflect light and throw minimal shadow. The communication function is most obvious in fresh water, where parr marks and bright colours serve as territorial signals among young fish, and in the distinctive breeding dress among spawning adults.

Points of thrust generation in swimming salmonid.

Internal organs include the basic structures common to other vertebrates. The single circulatory system is controlled by a simple two-part heart, the blood being pumped to the gills for exchange of waste carbon dioxide with oxygen, around the body by way of the blood vessels, and back to the heart via veins from the liver. The brain is the control centre of the nerve network; its pituitary body produces hormones which affect a variety of body functions. The stomach and intestinal tract secrete fluids which convert the digestible parts of food into proteins, fats and carbohydrates, while the liver converts sugars into glycogen for storage or transport via the blood, together with amino-acids and other nutrients, for maintenance and construction of cells throughout the body.

The kidney acts in eliminating digestive waste as well as excess water which builds up in fresh water as a result of osmotic pressures. In salt water, which is more saline than the body fluids, osmotic pressure acts in reverse; in the ocean salmonid fish maintain saline balance by drinking large amounts and excreting the excess salts through both faeces and gills.

ANGLING BASICS

Although the basic tackle of rod, line and hook has remained essentially the same since prehistoric times the past century has seen an unprecedented number of refinements. The industrial era which heralded the sport-fishing boom also produced a consumer industry in tackle and a constant flow of new products.

RODS Fishing rods, once made from varieties of natural wood, have been largely replaced by new materials combining strength and lightness. Built cane, developed in North America, became the standard item by the mid-twentieth century; created from cemented strips of tonkin cane, it is still preferred by many fly fishers for its natural character. The first popular synthetic material was glass fibre. Cheap, tough and very durable, glass rods remain the most widely used for most forms of angling. The latest material, carbon fibre or graphite, is a produce of space research which, thanks to its extreme lightness, is increasingly popular. Most fly fishing requires a specialised type of rod, whatever material is used in its construction.

REELS The main types include the centrepin, spinning, baitcasting and multiplier. The simple centrepin, which has been used for centuries, remains the standard item for fly fishing. Its limitation for other methods are its slow rate of retrieve and the difficulty of distance casting; its advantages include good fast-water line control and reliability in playing big fish. The fixed spool spinning reel, developed in England for low-water trout spinning, has become the most popular general purpose type. Its advantages are easy casting and fast retrieve; its main drawback is a tendency to cause line snag, especially for beginners. The closed-face baitcasting reel is basically similar to the spinning reel. Multipliers are used mainly for distance work with heavy weights.

LINES Once made from natural materials such as horsehair, silk and gut, modern lines are largely synthetic. Nylon monofilament is standard for bait and spin fishing and for fly leaders or tippets. Although relatively durable it is prone to abrasion and can rot; the last few yards should be checked regularly. Plastic fly lines come in numbered sizes and must be matched to individual rods for the necessary balance of rod and line.

FLY FISHING Fly techniques come under the general headings of wet fly, in which the fly is sunk, and dry fly, when it is floated on the surface. Outfits for the two styles are different in that dry fly fishing demands a stiffer rod, floating line and a relatively impermeable fly which is oiled frequently. Often regarded as the most pleasurable form of angling it is mainly used to take trout rising to surface insects. Wet fly fishing makes use of slow-, medium- or fast-sinking lines. Floating lines are also used, as in low water salmon fishing, when the fly is required to fish near the surface. Traditional wet fly work for trout involves casting the fly – usually a general insect

Knot tying is necessary in all forms of angling. Standard types include the blood knot (top) for joining lengths of nylon and the half-blood for attaching hooks etc. All knots should be well tested before fishing begins.

representation – and recovering line by hand. In running water the cast is normally made upsream – from behind the fish – except in high water conditions when down-and-across fishing can also be effective. Nymph fishing makes use of imitations of the larval or nymph stage of aquatic insects and is mostly used on fine tackle in clear lakes or streams. Another popular method, especially on big stillwaters, is the use of attractor flies or lures. A powerful rod and forward taper line or a shooting head, is often used to achieve distance. A big hairwing-type fly, stripped rapidly back towards the angler, achieves an effect similar to conventional spinning tactics.

Though sometimes regarded as a difficult art, the basics of fly casting can be learnt in an hour or two. As with other methods successful fishing relies largely on practice and a knowledge of fish behaviour. Fly fishing can be a useful adjunct to conservation; unlike bait or spin-caught fish those taken of fly are normally hooked lightly and, if released without any handling, will often recover.

SPINNING This covers the use of numerous artificial baits which attract fish by movement achieved by casting and retrieving, or by trolling behind a boat. Most represent small fish although the various spoons, spinners and plugs have little obvious resemblance to natural prey and may stimulate fish to strike by their eccentric colours and vibrations. Unlike natural baits, which can sometimes be fished in one area for long periods, spinning baits are likely to be taken quickly or not at all. When bank fishing for trout they are normally used on a roving basis, a few casts being made in each area before moving on. A tendency to catch on obstructions limits their use in weedy, snag-ridden or very shallow waters.

NATURAL BAITS The natural prey of salmonid fish provide a broad selection of natural baits. Unlike artificial fly or spinner they can be fished static or very slowly without being rejected and one or other of them can be used in most fishing situations.

The versatility of natural baits does not mean that they will catch more fish than artificials and regular results rely on skilful presentation and a choice of hook, bait and line sizes to suit water conditions and the mood of the fish. In clear streams trout and char will take best on light tackle and small baits including worms, insects, grubs or baitfish. Heavier gear and larger baits are more likely to succeed in flood water or under cover of darkness when fish are less likely to be choosy.

Natural baits can also be effective in tempting Atlantic salmon; although these fish do not feed in fresh water after their return from the sea they are often attracted to strike at worms, prawns, shrimps or small fish.

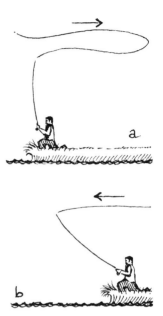

Basic fly casting. Easy as long as (a) the rod is stopped at the upright position on the back-cast and the line allowed to straighten behind and (b) the rod is then brought forward with a steady thrust aimed above the water; the line will they straighten before it settles.

FISHING RECORDS

INCHES-	LB. OZ.
9	- 5
10	- 7
11	- 9
12	- 12
13	- 15
14	1 - 3
15	1 - 7
16	1 -12
17	2 - 2
18	2 - 8
19	2 -15
20	3 - 7
21	4 - 0
22	4 - 9
23	5 - 3
24	5 - 15

Weight-for-length table for brown, rainbow or cutthroat trout in average summer condition. Variations up to 30% are not unusual. Fish are measured from snout to fork of tail.

Summary of author's trout catches, made over 7 seasons on a remote stream, provide a picture of the trout population. One year group (arrowed) was very low in numbers and resulted in the poor average sizes in years 2 and 3.

Although catch returns are mandatory on some rod fisheries the value of fishing diaries, whether for pleasure or water improvement, is often overlooked. Statistics collected by both individuals and organisations have many potential uses. A good diary can provide a rationale for the use of particular angling methods in different situations and an aid to understanding fish behaviour. It can also give a scientific assessment of the universal 'good old days' syndrome by providing facts and figures to show whether the fishing on a given water has actually declined and, if so, to what degree. More importantly, detailed catch figures can be used as a basis for fishery management. Good records will show, for instance, the productivity in terms of rod-hour effort as well as the size and numbers of fish. From these figures practical measures can be applied to enhance the fishery by the protection of certain year groups of fish, the development of a rational stocking policy or specific types of habitat improvement. Although angling records are unlikely to produce the sheer amount of facts of a professional survey they can, if kept over a number of seasons, produce enough for creative management.

On natural waters it is important to record the sizes of all fish caught, not just those over the size limit. Small ones do not necessarily need to be measured if they are obviously under the size limit; they can just be noted as 'small'. For ease of recording sizes can be further condensed into three or four categories corresponding approximately to the main year classes; these can be confirmed by scale reading. Experienced anglers should then be able to judge the categories by eye without having to measure every fish. Lengths are generally easier to record than weights and on the whole are more useful in telling the age of a fish.

While annual differences in the average size of fish caught, and the relative percentage of each year group, can usually be determined by recording lengths, the number of fishing hours should also be noted for calculation of rod-hour effort. It can also be useful to note the areas where catches are made, the angling methods used, and water conditions. A 'remarks' column can be added for weights, stomach contents or other details.

AGE	1+/2+	2+/3+	3+/4+	4+	AV. SIZE	TOTAL # FISH	MAX. WEIGHT
LENGTH	6"-8"	8-10	10-12	12+			
YEAR I	24%	46%	21%	9%	9½"	76	1lb.15oz.
II	50	23	22	5	8½	76	14oz.
III	57	32	5	6	7½	120	1lb. 1oz.
IV	34	41	21	4	9	80	1lb.12oz.
V	24	36	33	7	9½	74	3lb.1oz.
VI	18	47	27	8	9+	102	14oz.
VII	23	50	19	8	9½	114	1lb.4oz.
				TOTALS	AV. 9+	642	3lb.1oz.

Visual Records

Photos provide most catch records. Composing the subject needs as much attention as correct focus and lighting. More personal visual records include –

1. Dried heads. After hanging in a well-aerated outbuilding for a few weeks these can be varnished and mounted.

2. Outline drawings can make attractive wall decorations. A pencil line is drawn around the fish on good quality card and the final line, with addition of head details, made afterwards in ink. A wood panel with burn outline is also effective.

3. Gyo-taku print, a decorative record used by Japanese anglers. The fish is wiped dry and brushed over one side with ink or paint. An absorbent paper such as rice paper is then pressed over it. Eye details can be added afterwards.

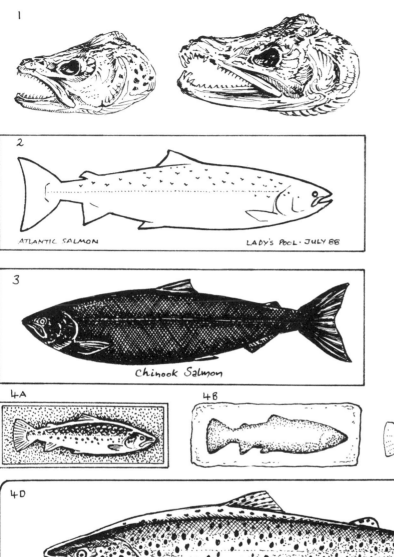

1

2

ATLANTIC SALMON   LADY'S POOL · JULY 88

3

Chinook Salmon

4A

4B

4C

4D

2lb.10oz.♂   · BROWN TROUT ·   WATER OF KEN

4. Plaster models are cheap and easy to make. The mould is made by lying the fish in a box of sand and pouring plaster over the exposed side. Flat-backed models can be taken straight from this first mould but fully 3-dimensional ones need a second mould made from the opposite side of the fish. Wires can be inserted before casting so that the model can be attached to a display board; models can also be hung as they are on a nail. Painting, a critical step in completing the model, can be done cheaply with artist's acrylics. Mixed with water these make effective, quick-drying washes for the background colours. Markings are added by mixing colours straight from the tube and using the actual fish, or a photo, as a guide to the size and location of the markings.

111

PREPARING THE CATCH

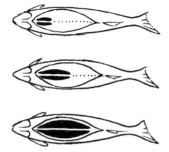

Gonads showing seasonal development of a maturing autumn spawner. From top: spring, undeveloped; summer, developing; autumn, fully developed.

The food value of all salmonid fish is excellent. They are easier to digest than meat and have similar protein and calorie content. They are particularly high in certain minerals including calcium, phosphorus and iron; sea-run fish also have a high iodine content. The fats which account for their richness are unsaturated.

Fish should be cleaned as soon as possible after killing to avoid the flesh becoming tainted by the spread of toxic bacteria or secretions from internal organs. The gutting stage can also be usefully combined with examination and recording of details such as weight, length, sex or stomach contents.

The sex of mature salmonids can be confirmed by the presence of whitish milt sacs in males and orange eggs in females. Immature males can be hard to identify since the milt is undeveloped; negative identification, however, is still possible since if a fish is an immature female small orange eggs are still discernible. The stomach contents of salmonids from fresh water often consist of a mass of small insects which can be identified by separating them in a saucer containing water; the addition of a little salt speeds the separation.

Freshly killed fish will deteriorate within hours at warm temperatures and those from fresh water are especially prone to bacterial infections. If cooled soon after killing and stored at near zero temperatures, however, they will keep for several days. Reliable signs of freshness include a clean smell, bright red gills and firm flesh. Domestic cats can be used to verify freshness; they will not normally touch a fish which is unsafe for human consumption. If in doubt as to edibility fish should either be discarded or else cooked right through and then kept at a high temperature for several minutes to destroy any harmful bacteria.

Freezing

Trout, salmon and char all freeze well. Their eating quality is only marginally impaired by freezing provided they are cooled rapidly,

Gutting

1. A shallow cut is made through the abdomen wall.

2. Innards are lifted together and severed as near to the head as possible.

3. Backbone is scored to remove kidney.

correctly packaged and kept no longer than a few months.

PREPARATION Fish for the freezer should be processed as soon as possible after killing. In order to avoid the flesh becoming tainted it is important to drain off excess blood and remove the gills plus any adhering membranes or fragments of internal organs. The body should be washed in cold, fresh water.

PACKAGING It is vital to keep frozen fish in air-and water-tight materials such as polythene or freezer gauge foil. Freezer burn, which results in loss of flavour, is caused by moisture loss via air spaces in the packaging; it can be prevented by tight wrapping or by sucking air out of freezer bags before closing. When steaks or fillets are stored together they can first be wrapped separately in waxed or greaseproof paper for easy separation after thawing.

Slow freezing causes loss of flavour and texture. Packages should therefore be placed at the bottom of the freezer or use made of a quick freezing facility. Large amounts should not be put in at one time since they will raise the temperature and take longer to freeze.

Thawing is best done by leaving packages in a refrigerator for a day or in cold water for a few hours; fish thawed at room temperature lose both flavour and food value. They should be completely defrosted before use and once thawed, not refrozen.

STORAGE LIFE Under normal storage conditions salmonids keep well for about four months. Storage life can be extended to seven or eight months – and the appearance of the fish preserved – by covering with a layer of ice before packaging. For large whole fish this can be done by freezing and then dipping in cold water to form an ice glaze. The dipping is repeated until a continuous thick coating is formed; the fish is then packaged in the usual way. The storage life of steaks or fillets can be similarly extended by freezing in airtight containers filled with fresh water.

Filleting

1. A cut is made close along the backbone; at the front end the flesh needs to be scraped clear of the projecting ribs.

2. The process is repeated on the opposite side.

113

COOKING

Salmonid fish are best cooked simply to maintain the fine flavour and texture for which they are renowned. Heavy spicing or strong sauces disguise flavour and are of value only for some farm-reared fish or specimens in poor condition.

FRYING Shallow frying is ideal for freshwater-dwelling trout or char. These fish, especially the small ones, lack the heavy oil content of sea-run salmonids and frying in butter or oil can improve their eating qualities. Those under 12 inches (30 cm) are best fried whole; when used fresh a little salt sprinkled in the body cavity a few hours before cooking will get rid of any residual taints and enhance sweetness. Fish over 12 inches or so are best filleted since they are too thick for convenient pan frying.

The skin of small trout and char is delicious when fried golden brown. Coating them helps achieve overall crispness; they can be rolled in semolina, which has good covering capacity, or in the traditional oatmeal, breadcrumbs or flour. They should be fried hot and fast; two or three minutes on each side is normally enough.

Deep frying is suitable for all species but again is most appropriate for fish with a relatively low fat content. Batter is the standard coating for deep frying and for best results the fat should be pre-heated to at least 400°F (210°C) and the fish fried until golden brown.

POACHING AND STEAMING These methods are particularly suited to salmon and other sea-run species whose rich flesh does not benefit from the addition of oil or fat. Light cooking in water or steam is also a sure way of preserving the delicacy of flavour and texture.

Whole fish can be poached in a fish kettle containing a removal rack. Alternatively a normal covered stewpan can be used with the fish, or sections of it, wrapped in cheesecloth. A saucer can be used to keep the package off the bottom of the pan and careful removal in the cloth will keep the flesh from breaking open. The fish should be just covered in cold water, to which a little salt and lemon juice has been added, or in cold bouillon. The liquid is brought to boiling point and simmered very gently; some prefer to keep the temperature just below boiling. Cooking time will vary according to the thickness of the fish. If it is to be served cold it can be left to cool in the liquid.

Steaming can be done in a steamer or in a pressure cooker, each fish or section being first covered in buttered paper. A little salt and pepper, plus lemon juice or vinegar, are normally added. For pressure cooking the trivet is normally greased and half a pint (280 ml) of water used; cooking time is 6–8 minutes for steaks and 10–12 minutes for larger cuts.

BAKING OR BROILING These methods are ideal for whole fish cooked in a baking dish or wrapped in foil. Small fish or steaks are best broiled or braised by adding a small amount of water or stock; medium-sized ones can be baked with a little butter. Large, oily fish need only be baked with a little seasoning and basted when necessary with their own juices.

BARBECUEING AND GRILLING All salmonid fish are suitable for grilling or barbecueing. A light covering of butter will prevent the skins drying out; large fish should be scored before cooking.

Open air cooking has a special appeal and fish cooked by the waterside, fresh after capture, provide a unique taste experience. The camper should be able to pan fry his catch but the angler out for a day's fishing can make do without any cooking materials – a sharp knife is the only utensil needed. Trout, salmon and char are delicious barbecued on the hot coals of a hardwood campfire; spitted on green peeled branches placed near the flames; or simply baked on hot stones. All species have sufficient fat content to prevent their flesh becoming too dry and the smoke from hardwoods does well in place of normal seasoning.

SMOKING Home smoking can be done in a wooden box or metal drum covered with a cloth, or in a purpose-built hut with fireproof floor, mesh screens or fish racks, and ventilation holes at the top. In both cases the fire is normally placed outside and the smoke led in through a pipe. A smouldering woodchip or sawdust fire can be built 2 or 3 ft (½–1 metre) away from the fish but normal wood fires should be 5–10 ft (1.5–3 metres) away. Most hardwoods – but not conifers – are good for smoking; favourites are alder, hickory and oak. Peat or sphagnum moss can also be used. Hot and cold smoking are the basic methods. The first step in both is to coat the fish well in salt to retard the spread of toxic bacteria. Dry salt can be rubbed over the whole fish which should be fresh, gutted, and with gills removed. A standard curing mixture consisting of four parts salt, two parts brown sugar, and two tablespoons each of black pepper and bay leaves can be used instead of plain salt. Alternatively the fish can be left in a brine solution – four cups of salt to a gallon of water – then removed and left until the salt glaze dries.

Hot smoking, the common method, involves smoking the fish for 8–10 hours, the temperature starting around 43°C (110°F) and increasing to 80°C (180°F). Hot smoked fish will only keep for a few days without refridgeration or freezing.

Cold smoking requires longer salt applications and is carried out for several days at under 32°C (90°F). Cold smoked fish are stronger in flavour, drier, and will keep considerably longer.

FISH KEEPING

HOME AQUARIA All species can be kept in aquaria. Rainbow trout are especially suitable thanks to their easy domestication and wide availability; chars are also easily tamed but brown trout retain a natural shyness. Water temperatures for all species should be kept below 20°C (69°F) and their high oxygen requirement means that an air pump is usually needed. Very small aquaria are not suitable although they can be useful for fly-tying enthusiasts in the study of aquatic insects important in trout diet.

GARDEN PONDS Trout do well in garden ponds provided the water is kept cool and there are sufficient submerged aquatic plants to provide oxygen. Ponds can be constructed using waterproofed concrete or linings such as heavy-gauge rubber or polythene sheeting. If quantities of fish are to be raised in small ponds for eating purposes, additional oxygenation may be required via an air pump or a constant water inflow and regular feeding carried out with commercial-quality foods.

FARMING Trout farming, a relatively new agricultural practice, has grown rapidly into a major industry. Today it is often specialised with some operations concentrating on production of eggs, fry or larger fish. Although fully domestic strains have yet to be developed the easily tamed, fast-growing rainbow trout has given rise to semi-domestic types; this species is virtually the only trout widely raised for eating. Salmon farming, a more recent development, relies largely on Atlantic salmon, coho and chinook. Other species of trout, salmon or char as well as hybrids are raised for specialised food markets or stocking angling waters.

Hatcheries rely on a constant supply of very pure water, a supply of brood fish or eggs, and a hatchery unit which parallels conditions required for development of eggs in nature. At the active feeding stage fry are transferred to shallow ponds or to tanks with feed hoppers supplying food in pellet form at regular intervals. The young grow at different rates and a large part of fish farming comprises the laborious process of grading, with fish of similar sizes being regularly sorted and transferred to their own ponds or cages. Trout are sold fresh, frozen or smoked, mainly at portion sizes of about 8oz.

The economics of intensive rearing dictate the keeping of a maximum weight of fish in a given space. Rainbow trout are kept at up to 4 lbs per cubic foot (33 lb per cubic metre); even at half this density, however, they can be prone to stress which leads to development of disease or parasite infection, the causative organisms of which are already present in most waters. Successful fish farming relies not only on good husbandry but on a knowledge of disease prevention and cure.

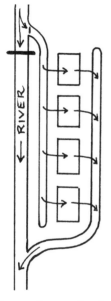

Layout of conventional earth ponds showing controlled water flow. Trout and salmon are also reared in floating net cages in lakes or ocean inlets.

COMMERCIAL FISHING

The last great natural hunting resource on earth, fish remain abundant enough to provide a major food source for humans and the basis of the world's largest participant sport. Of all fish types the salmonids are one of the most valuable due to their high demand as food as well as their importance in angling. Commercial fishing, which was for thousands of years carried out primarily in fresh waters, is now concentrated more on the oceans and in particular the inshore approaches to salmon rivers.

SALTWATER FISHING A large proportion of Pacific and Atlantic salmon are taken in seine and gill nets. One type of gill net, the monofilament drift net, is practically invisible to fish and several miles of it can be set and hauled relatively easily; its deadliness has posed such threats to salmon stocks, however, that it is increasingly becoming banned or its use regulated by catch limits and quotas.

Hook and line fishing is also important. Some Atlantic salmon fisheries are based on long lines employing thousands of baited hooks while commercial trolling is a major technique for chinook, coho and sockeye salmon in the Pacific. Other methods include the many traditional types of traps and nets used at river mouths. In several parts of the world similar small-scale methods are used in subsistence fisheries; salmon are a winter staple for many North American coastal Indians and Arctic char are important to the Inuit and to rural peoples in Siberia.

FRESHWATER FISHING In some areas freshwater fisheries remain important. In the big lakes of northern Canada the lake trout is a major commercial species while many coastal rivers support subsistence fisheries for salmon or char. In Siberian rivers a commercial fishery is based on the Arctic char and the big freshwater-dwelling taimen is also locally exploited. Angling plays a significant part in food production; millions of rod-caught trout and salmon are eaten worldwide every year and some anglers pay towards the cost of their sport by sale of catches.

STATUS In the past century many freshwater fisheries have been lost. Habitat destruction, the development of trout farming and the preservation of waters for angling have all contributed to their demise. The expansion of ocean fishing has resulted in the creation of new salmon fisheries, although many of these are now under pressure. Increasing catch restrictions resulting from over-fishing, the current boom in salmon farming, and moves to preserve stocks for the rod fisheries have resulted in the difficulties faced by many traditional coastal operations as well as the ocean fleets. The total salmon resource is so large, however, that as long as rivers remain healthy and good spawning escapements are allowed to reach them a surplus of quality wild fish is always likely to be taken for human consumption.

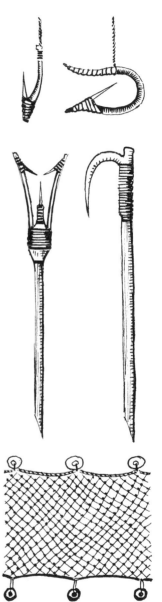

Stone age fishing tools were highly developed. Hook and line, spear and gaff, and nets of braided fibre are still in use today.

FISHERY MANAGEMENT

The need for management has been created by human pressures on fish stocks. In many industrialised areas natural waters can only survive under creative administration. Even wilderness regions need local protective measures or monitoring for water acidification while in the oceans cooperation between nations is a necessity. Today the management of salmonids takes place at local, national and international levels.

A good understanding of the concept of fish year groups is fundamental to fishery management. Meaningful enhancement measures can only be applied when the growth rates and age compositions of fish stocks are known. The necessary samples can be obtained from complete catch records see (see page 110) or by electro-fishing a stretch of water; ages and growth rates can be deduced from scale reading. Once some basic information has been aquired enhancement policies can be checked at intervals by examining catch records to ascertain any changes in stock density, growth rates, or rod-hour effort.

On trout waters management is often seen purely in terms of stocking and restocking. Where spawning grounds are lacking or angling pressure exceptionally heavy the planting of hatchery trout is the only way of maintaining a fishery. The carrying capacity of every water is limited, however, by the food supply, and, where spawning is adequate, it will be fully taken up by native fish even when a good proportion is taken by angling. Stock fish commonly move downstream or starve; various studies have shown that on natural trout streams they normally add little if anything to catch returns. They can in fact be damaging to a fishery by competing with, or interbreeding with, the more desirable wild trout which are better adapted to their own water.

Habitat improvement is the best way of enhancing natural stocks. The angling quality of shallow trout streams, for instance, can be quickly raised by the creation of rough stone or timber dams. The current will scour out the bed below them, making pools in which larger trout will soon grow. Unproductive stretches of salmon rivers can similarly be improved by building simple stone groynes to create holding spots, and where breeding grounds are poor they can be created by laying beds of appropriately sized gravel in stream pools. On stillwaters productivity can be increased by the establishment of suitable plants and insects, the introduction of small forage fish or periodic flooding of the surrounds.

Rough stone or timber dams greatly improve fishing on shallow trout streams. The pool created upstream is temporary, becoming filled with stones by the current, but the one scoured below becomes permanent if the dam is built strong enough to withstand winter floods.

RESEARCH

Fisheries research is divided into two types – applied research, which is aimed at solving specific problems, and pure research which is concerned with increasing the overall knowledge of fish or their environment. Both may involve work on fish biology and population dynamics or environmental studies based in limnology, the study of freshwaters, or oceanography, the study of the oceans. Pure research is conducted largely at educational or research institutes while applied research is more the concern of government fishery departments.

POPULATION STUDIES Scale reading and tagging are two of the basic techniques used in the study of salmonid populations. When examined under a strong magnifying glass or low-power microscope fish scales reveal a series of annual rings like those of tree sections. Dark winter bands are composed of narrowly spaced rings formed during the period of slow winter growth; uneven spawning marks are sometimes detectable as well. Scales can be used to determine age, growth rate and length of time spent in fresh or salt water, while back-calculations can also reveal the size of a fish at different life stages. By reading a number of scales a picture can be built up of age, spawning habits and migratory patterns of trout and salmon populations. Scales from these two types of fish can usually be read with a fair amount of accuracy, but those of char, are not so easy. The life details of char are more usually obtained from reading otoliths (inner ear bones) or the large bones of the gill cover.

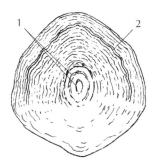

Scale of Atlantic salmon grilse. 1. Two winter bands in juvenile fresh water stage. 2. Single winter band in ocean phase indicates 1+ years in salt water. Total age 3+.

Simple tagging, which was used as long ago as Isaac Walton's time, provides useful information on fish migrations. Radio tagging, a recent development, enables local movements to be followed precisely and is mainly used to track the progress of anadromous adults in fresh water.

HABITAT STUDIES These include the study of water types, foods and their relationship to fish. Food chains and the value of individual prey items are important in understanding, and sometimes influencing, growth rates since size and numbers of fish rely on the availability of specific types of prey at different life stages.

Studies in water temperature and chemistry can indicate the potential for success of different species or of their prey. Char, for instance, do better in relatively cold water while alkalinity and acidity are major influences on all species.

GENETIC RESEARCH Advances in molecular biology have promoted a more precise understanding of relationships between genera, species and races than was possible by conventional physical comparisons. The counting of chromosomes, for instance, ascertained that the Caspian salmon was in fact a giant race of brown trout. More recent techniques of protein analysis have provided fine measurements of genetic variations and have shown that individual waters commonly hold their own genetic strains.

SPECIES NAMES

Official name	Other names, including local names and different life stages
ATLANTIC SALMON *Salmo salar*	Salmon which have spent a single winter at sea are commonly known as grilse. Larger, older salmon are often prefixed by a seasonal name: spring, summer, autumn salmon.
PACIFIC SALMONS	
COHO *Oncorhynchus kisutch*	Silver Salmon, Blueback, Northern Coho.
CHINOOK *O. tshawytscha*	King Salmon, Spring Salmon, Quinnat Salmon, Tyee.
SOCKEYE *O. nerka*	Blueback, Red Salmon.
CHUM *O. keta*	Dog Salmon.
PINK *O. gorbuscha*	Humpback Salmon.
MASU *O. masou*	Cherry Salmon.
BROWN TROUT,	German Brown, Loch Leven Trout, Ferox, Gillaroo, Sonaghan.
SEA TROUT *Salmo trutta*	Sewin, White Trout, Peal, Sea-run Brown Trout, Caspian Salmon, Aral Trout, Finnock, Whitling, Herling, Slob Trout (estuary-dwelling fish).
RAINBOW TROUT,	Kamloops Trout.
STEELHEAD *Salmo gairdnerii*	Chromer, Half-pounder, Sea-run Rainbow Trout.
CUTTHROAT TROUT *Salmo clarkii*	Harvest Trout (anadromous fish). Inland forms are sometimes called Native Trout; important races may be prefixed by local terms, e.g. Lahontan Cutthroat.
RARE TROUT AND HYBRIDS	see pages 75, 82–89
CHARS	
BROOK TROUT *Salvelinus fontinalis*	Brook Char, Eastern Brook Trout, Speckled trout, Native Trout, Aurora Trout, Dublin Pond Char. Anadromous fish are often called Salters or Sea Trout.
LAKE TROUT *S. namaycush*	Lake Char, Grey Trout, Togue, Mackinaw.
ARCTIC CHAR *S. alpinus*	Marston Trout, Blueback Trout, Sunapee Trout, Windermere Char.
DOLLY VARDEN *S. malma*	Bull Trout, Pacific Char.
EAST ASIAN CHAR *S. leucomaensis*	Japanese Char.
TAIMEN *Hucho taimen*	Siberian Taimen.
HUCHEN *Hucho hucho*	Danubian Salmon.

INDEX